Challenge

Science

KS3: Year 9

Age 13–14

Mark Edwards

Introduction

One of the most powerful things about science is its ability to explain many different things using just a few ideas. This book challenges you to use your scientific knowledge to explore all sorts of different situations. The questions are not only designed to give you a thorough revision of all the topics from the Key Stage 3 National Curriculum but also to extend your knowledge and understanding and to get you thinking like a scientist.

Each topic begins with a few practice questions. These introduce you to the ideas and the scientific words that you need to use in the later questions. If you struggle with the practice questions then either move to a new topic or go back to your revision guide (try our *Revise KS3* series). The 'challenge' questions range in difficulty. Some are standard questions that you might see in an exam. Others encourage you to look up further information. A few are designed to really stretch your mind. Don't worry: if all else fails, there are detailed answers at the back of the book. Good luck!

First published 2007
exclusively for WHSmith by
Hodder Murray, an imprint of Hodder Education
and a member of the Hodder Headline Group,
an Hachette Livre UK Company, 338 Euston Road, London NW1 3BH

Impression number 10 9 8 7 6 5 4 3 2 1
Year 2011 2010 2009 2008 2007
Text and illustrations © Hodder Education 2007

A CIP record for this book is available from the British Library.

Text: Mark Edwards
Cover illustration: Sally Newton Illustrations

Typeset by Servis Filmsetting Ltd., Manchester

ISBN 978 0 340 94562 9

Printed and bound in Spain.

Contents

1: Inheritance and cloning

You will revise:
 - inherited characteristics through sexual reproduction
 - dominant and recessive genes
 - what we mean by a clone and how we can produce them.

Get started

Organisms of the same species have characteristics that are different from each other. Offspring can inherit different characteristics from the same parents. Organisms that are clones of each other are genetically identical.

Practice

1. What are gametes?

2. How are sperm and egg cells adapted for their roles in reproduction?

3. What are genes? Where would you find them in a cell?

4. Why is your genetic make-up more similar to your parents' than to your grandparents'?

Challenge

5. a Explain how sexual reproduction leads to offspring with characteristics from both the mother and the father.

   b Why do brothers and sisters have some characteristics that are similar but other characteristics that are very different?

   c Describe how fertilisation can lead to identical and non-identical twins.

   d Is it possible for two sisters to have the same genetic make-up even if they are not identical twins? Explain your answer.

6. In 1865, Mendel discovered how certain characteristics are inherited by pea plants. He investigated dwarf pea plants and tall pea plants.

   Here are the results.

Gene from mother plant	Gene from father plant	Offspring
Dwarf	Dwarf	Always dwarves
Dwarf	Tall	Always tall
Tall	Dwarf	Always tall
Tall	Tall	Always tall

   a Explain why the gene responsible for a plant being tall is called a dominant gene.

Mendel suggested that each plant inherited one gene (either tall or dwarf) from the mother and one gene from the father. So an offspring has two tall/dwarf genes.

b Explain why a parent plant must be tall if it passes on the 'tall' gene but it can either be tall or a dwarf if it passes on the 'dwarf' gene.

c Two tall parents produce a dwarf offspring. What combinations of genes must both parents have?

7 **a** What is a clone?

b How can you clone plants?

c Explain why single-celled amoebae are clones of each other.

One way to produce a clone is to completely remove the nucleus from an egg and replace it with the nucleus from a cell of another individual. This behaves like a normal fertilised egg and, in the right conditions, will develop into a new organism.

d Is the new organism a clone of the organism that produced the egg or a clone from the organism that produced the nucleus?

e Why is it theoretically possible to produce a clone from almost any cell of your body?

f Suggest two reasons why not many mammals have been cloned so far.

8 There are millions of tiny structures called ribosomes in your cells. What is their role in using the genetic information stored in the DNA?

9 Mitochondria are structures inside your cells that produce energy. They also contain DNA but this is cloned directly from your mother. Explain why the DNA in the mitochondria of a complete stranger is likely to be very nearly identical to the mitochondrial DNA in you.

10 The DNA in the nucleus of your cells is split up into pairs of chromosomes. Describe how the chromosomes determine what gender you are.

How did I do?

I can describe the difference between identical and non-identical twins in terms of their genetic make-up. ☐

I can explain how siblings can have very different characteristics even though they have the same parents. ☐

I can draw diagrams to show how we can produce a clone by replacing the nucleus of an egg. ☐

2: Variation and selection

You will revise:

- environmental and genetic causes of variation
- natural and artificial selection
- the difference between a species and a breed
- genetic modification.

Get started

You've seen that variation within a species can arise from both environmental and genetic factors. Natural and artificial selection can result in some of these different characteristics passing down the generations but other characteristics can die out altogether.

Practice

1   Discuss whether the height of a tree is an inherited or an environmental characteristic.

2   Suggest two reasons why tomatoes have increased in size over the last few centuries.

3   Explain how selective breeding has resulted in domestic dogs.

4   What is the difference between a species and a breed?

Challenge

5   a What is meant by natural selection?

    b Explain how bacteria that are resistant to antibiotics are naturally selected in hospitals. Why is this a problem?

    c Why does selection occur with bacteria more obviously than with other organisms over a certain time period?

    d Explain how a species can become more and more adapted to its environment.

    e Suggest how Darwin's observations of finches added weight to the evidence for his theory of evolution by natural selection.

6   A farmer has a female cow that is good at producing milk, and a bull that produces a lot of meat.

    a Suggest how the farmer could produce a cow that is both good at producing milk but also produces good meat over several generations.

    b State one other characteristic that farmers would try to encourage by selective breeding.

7 **a** For centuries there has been a close relationship between humans and the domesticated dog. Explain why this has led to many distinct breeds of dog.

b Suggest why large breeds of dogs tend to be much more docile (gentler) than small breeds of dogs.

8 **a** Describe how you can make clones of geraniums.

b Why would this method of producing geraniums be no good if you wanted to improve a certain characteristic (e.g. colour of flowers)?

c If you had a collection of geraniums, how might you be able to produce a new breed of geranium?

9 **a** How can a successful male (stallion) racehorse continue to earn lots of money after he has retired from racing?

b Why is it important to study the characteristics of the mare carefully before choosing an appropriate stallion for breeding purposes?

c Suggest why the total horse population used to include a much higher percentage of the stronger breeds than it does today.

10 We have now learnt to enhance certain characteristics of crops (such as their yield or nutritional value) by genetically modifying them.

a State one similarity and one difference between genetic modification and selective breeding.

b Some people are worried about genetically modified (GM) crops. Suggest a cause for concern with using this new technology.

c State two advantages of using GM crops.

11 Sometimes the genetic make-up of a particular cell can spontaneously change. What do we call this change and how can this lead to the development of a new species?

12 After the dog, the goat was the earliest animal to be domesticated. By considering the diet of goats, suggest why they became a valuable source of food.

How did I do?

I can explain the difference between artificial and natural selection. ☐

I can suggest a breeding programme to develop a breed that has desirable characteristics. ☐

I can discuss the advantages and disadvantages of genetic modification. ☐

3: Keeping fit and healthy

You will revise:
- effective breathing and respiration in fit people
- healthy bones and joints
- the dangers of smoking.

Get started

The body has many systems which need to work together effectively. These systems can become less effective with aging and with an unhealthy lifestyle.

Practice

1. Explain the difference between being fit and being healthy.

2. Write down the word equation and the symbol equation for respiration.

3. Briefly describe the systems of the body that deliver the reactants of respiration to the cells and then remove the products.

4. What are the similarities and differences between a stroke and a heart attack?

Challenge

5. a What organ is responsible for creating blood pressure?

   b Why do people who have low blood pressure often feel faint and lack energy?

   c Explain how cholesterol lining the insides of your blood vessels increases blood pressure.

   d What might eventually happen to the blood vessels if you have high blood pressure?

6. This question is about the effect that smoking has on health.

   a Why do people become addicted to smoking?

   b Explain the normal function of ciliated epithelial cells that line the air passages.

   c Smoking can stop the cilia beating properly. How does this lead to a smoker's cough?

   d State two reasons why smokers can become permanently short of oxygen.

e Some chemicals in inhaled smoke are carcinogenic. What disease could these chemicals cause?

f Explain how a mother smoking when she is pregnant could have an adverse effect on the fetus.

7 a How do the diaphragm and the intercostal muscles act to make us breathe in?

b Which takes more effort: breathing in or breathing out? Explain why.

c When you exercise, why do you breathe more deeply and why does the heart beat faster?

8 This question is about the bones in your body.

a State three functions of the skeleton.

b What is the difference in the way tendons and ligaments are connected?

c Explain the purpose of synovial fluid in a joint.

This is a diagram of the elbow joint.

d Why do you need two muscles to control this joint?

e Describe what happens to the muscles in order to lift the forearm up and then bring it back down.

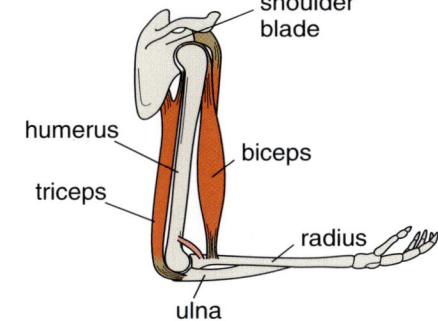

f Your bones act as levers.
Instead of multiplying the forces (like most levers) these levers multiply the distances. Therefore the distance the arm moves is much further than the distance the muscle moves. What advantage was this in our distant past?

9 a Explain how your body respires when there is not enough oxygen.

b Why do you continue to breathe heavily for a while after you have exercised?

How did I do?

	✔
I can describe the processes of respiration and breathing and how this leads to effective cell function.	☐
I can explain the difference between muscles, tendons and ligaments and why we always need at least two muscles for a particular joint.	☐
I can describe the biological dangers of smoking.	☐

4: Diet and drugs

You will revise:
- problems associated with diet
- calculating the body mass index
- methods of researching new drugs
- use and misuse of recreational drugs.

Get started

Your body has to deal with any material that enters it. Most material (such as a balanced diet and prescribed drugs) does the body good. However, other material can cause harm.

Practice

1 State the five principle components of a balanced diet.

2 State two factors that are leading to a more obese society. Suggest how these factors have arisen in recent years.

3 Why can drinking alcohol be far more dangerous than just a risk to long-term health?

4 What do we mean by the terms *addiction* and *tolerance* when we talk about drugs?

Challenge

5 Listed below are some diseases to do with diet. For each disease state how a change in diet could alleviate the symptoms:

a Diabetes   b Scurvy   c Obesity

d Anaemia   e Constipation   f Kwashiorkor

g Which of these diseases are not caused by a poor diet?

6 Your body mass index (BMI) can be used as a guide to whether you are under- or overweight. To calculate your BMI you divide your mass (in kg) by your height (in m) squared. A BMI of less than 20 is classed as underweight; between 20 and 25 is classed as normal; between 25 and 30 is overweight and over 30 is obese.

a Copy and complete this table.

Mass (kg)	Height (m)	BMI (kg/m^2)	Weight category
50	1.50	22.2	Normal
60	1.75		
70	1.50		
90	1.80		

b Why might some sports men and women be classed as overweight on this scale when they are actually at their ideal weight?

7 **a** Suggest why the recommended limit for alcohol per week is about 1.5 times as much for men as it is for women.

b Explain why the legal limit of alcohol in the blood for a pilot is a quarter of what it is for a car driver.

c It takes 1 hour for the liver to turn 1 unit of alcohol into harmless substances. If someone drinks 6 pints of beer then how long does it take the body to reduce the alcohol in the blood to the legal limit? (A pint of beer contains 2 units of alcohol. Assume the legal limit is 3 units.)

d What is cirrhosis of the liver? Why is this often a fatal condition?

8 A pharmaceutical company is trialling a new drug. They are doing a 'double-blind' trial which means that neither the researchers nor the patients know whether the medicine they are taking is the real drug or just a placebo.

a What is a placebo? Why is it important to include this in the trial?

b Explain why it adds weight to the evidence if the doctors observing the welfare of the patients don't know whether the medicine is real or not.

c Many drugs are tested on animals first. Suggest why.

9 **a** Recreational drugs can be grouped into four categories. Stimulants and sedatives are two of them. What are the other two categories?

b Give an example of a drug in each category.

c As well as health problems to the user, how do drugs often cause social problems?

10 **a** Why does possessing class A drugs result in much tougher punishments than possessing class C drugs?

b Drugs can be very dangerous. Under what circumstances do doctors prescribe some of these drugs for legal use?

11 What is the difference between becoming physically dependent and psychologically dependent on a drug? Which one of these dependencies does a nicotine patch deal with?

How did I do?

I can calculate my body mass index and use it to determine my weight category. ☐

I can explain what we mean by a double-blind trial. ☐

I can describe what we mean by addiction and tolerance. ☐

I can discuss a particular recreational drug (e.g. alcohol) and the issues associated with it. ☐

5: Photosynthesis

You will revise:
- the chemical reaction of photosynthesis
- experimental evidence for photosynthesis
- factors that affect the rate of the reaction.

Get started

Plants can convert energy from the Sun into chemical energy by photosynthesis. The plants themselves use this energy in respiration but some of the energy is passed up the food chain. As well as providing us with energy in a useful form it also produces the oxygen we breathe.

Practice

1. Photosynthesis can be split up into two words: *photo* and *synthesis*. Explain how these words describe the chemical reaction.

2. Describe the standard tests for oxygen, carbon dioxide and starch.

3. How are photosynthesis and respiration related?

4. What is meant by biomass?

Challenge

5. a Write down the word equation and the symbol equation for photosynthesis.

   b This reaction needs energy to work. Where does this energy come from?

   c In terms of the energy involved, explain the role of the chlorophyll in the leaves.

6. This question is about growing an orange tree in a tub of soil.

   a Every year, the orange tree gains mass and the soil loses mass. However, the amount of mass the tree gains is thousands of times more than the mass the soil loses. Suggest where this extra mass has come from.

   b Why does the mass of the soil decrease a little (assuming that the water content remains the same)?

7. a When you are carrying out experiments to investigate photosynthesis, why do you sometimes need to de-starch the plant?

   b De-starching plants involves putting them in darkness for a few days. Explain what happens to the starch.

Once the plants have been de-starched you can carry out your investigation. One way of detecting photosynthesis is by looking for new starch that has been formed in the leaves.

c By considering the difference between plant cells and animal cells, explain why placing iodine on the leaves of a plant has no effect.

d How does boiling the leaves in water and then applying hot ethanol allow the iodine test to work? (Hint: chlorophyll is insoluble in water.)

e Describe how you can heat up ethanol safely.

8 Here is a diagram showing some pondweed photosynthesising in some water.

a From where does the pondweed get the carbon dioxide that it needs for photosynthesis?

b Suggest how you could investigate how the rate of photosynthesis depends on light intensity.

c State two control variables in this investigation and explain why they need to be controlled.

d Why would an oxygen probe and a datalogger be very useful for this investigation?

e Sketch a graph to show how the rate of photosynthesis depends on light intensity.

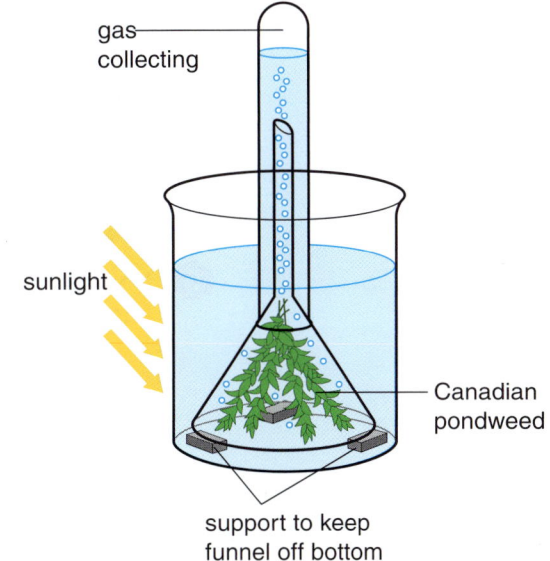

gas collecting

sunlight

Canadian pondweed

support to keep funnel off bottom

9 What is happening when the levels of oxygen and carbon dioxide remain the same near the leaves of a living plant?

10 Oxygen was naturally in the atmosphere when the Earth was formed. However, it did not stay in the atmosphere for long. What happened to it?

11 Explain why oxygen in a planet's atmosphere would suggest that the planet harbours life.

How did I do?

	✔
I can write a word equation for photosynthesis.	☐
I can describe an experiment to demonstrate photosynthesis in variegated leaves.	☐
I can explain why photosynthesis in plants is vital for human life.	☐

6: Leaves and roots

You will revise:

- the tissue structure of leaves and roots
- how these structures help photosynthesis
- transporting chemicals inside the plants.

Get started

The leaves and roots of a plant are both organs that perform specific functions. Leaves are involved in photosynthesis and roots in obtaining water and minerals from the soil (as well as holding the plant in place).

Practice

1. Why do the cells on the top side of leaves have many more chloroplasts than the cells on the bottom?

2. Explain the advantage of leaves having a large surface area.

3. Why are leaves and roots organs rather than tissues or systems?

4. Why do leaves need a large supply of water?

Challenge

5. You can investigate where photosynthesis takes place by using variegated leaves.

   a What is a variegated leaf?

   b Describe how you can show that photosynthesis takes place only in the green sections of the leaf.

6. a The veins in a leaf provide structure to keep the leaf rigid. What is their role in photosynthesis?

   b Little openings called stomata are present on the underside of the leaf. Why are they open during the day and closed during the night?

   c Above the stomata are little air spaces within the leaf. Suggest what these are for.

   d The stomata in the leaves regulate the amount of water loss. Suggest why the upper layer of the leaf has a waxy surface.

   e Why is the distance between the top and the bottom of the leaf usually very small?

7. One product of photosynthesis in a leaf is glucose. As well as for respiration, it has a wide range of uses within the plant.

   a Why is glucose converted into starch?

b Glucose is often converted into other sugars such as fructose. This makes their fruits nice to eat. What is the advantage of this to the plant?

c Amino acids are formed from glucose combining with other elements such as nitrogen. Where do these other elements come from? Why are amino acids so important?

d Glucose can be turned into a carbohydrate called cellulose. What part of the plant cell is made from this material?

e The cell membranes are made from fats (again, made from glucose). What is the role of the membrane in cell function?

8 Here is a diagram of a root.

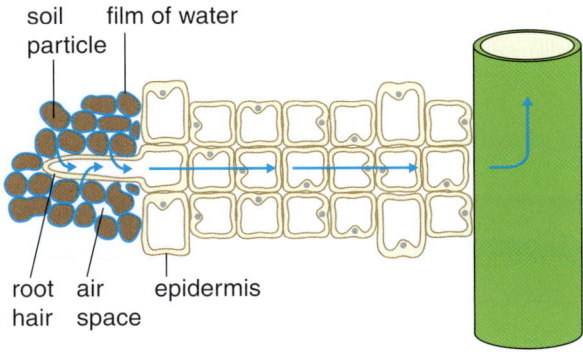

soil particle   film of water

root hair   air space   epidermis

a There are hundreds of root hairs per square centimetre of root. In what way does this help the function of the root?

b Why are there no chloroplasts in the root cells?

c Root cells need to respire. Where do they get their oxygen from?

d Why do plants need minerals as well as water?

e Water enters the cells by diffusion but the minerals need active transport. Suggest which one of these methods requires some of the plant's energy.

9 What is the role of the xylem and the phloem in plant function? How is this role performed in the human body?

10 Some plants in mineral-deficient habitats have developed a different way of obtaining minerals rather than using the soil. What sort of plants are these?

How did I do?

✔

I can draw diagrams of typical leaf and a root cells. ☐

I can explain how the cells are adapted for their particular function. ☐

I can describe the difference in the tissue found on the top of a leaf compared to the bottom of a leaf. ☐

7: Food from plants

You will revise:
- food from different parts of a plant
- cereal crops and legume plants
- the carbon cycle.

Get started

Plants are always at the beginning of the food chain and are therefore responsible for all of the food that we eat. Not only do they provide us with energy, they can also give us the chemicals that we need to produce and maintain our bodies.

Practice

1. What is the name for organisms that eat both plants and animals?

2. Humans can be tertiary consumers. By considering food chains, explain what this means.

3. What happens to the amount of energy that gets passed down the food chain? Explain your answer.

4. Why is the biomass of the producers (plants) in a habitat much larger than the biomass of tertiary consumers?

Challenge

5. a From a plant's perspective, what is the purpose of a fruit?

   b What is the difference between a dry and a succulent fruit.

   c What process triggers a flower to turn into a fruit?

   d Explain how succulent fruits, in particular, can provide us with a lot of energy.

6. a List four types of cereal crop.

   b Which class of plant do cereals belong to?

   c Explain why cereals have gradually produced much bigger yields over the last ten thousand years.

   d Our bodies don't digest bran (the husk of the fruit produced by wheat). Why is it still included in full-fibre breakfasts?

   e In what way do most of us consume hay and silage for breakfast?

7 **a** List three types of legume plant.

   b Identify the plants in your list where we eat both the fruit and the seeds together and identify the plants where we only eat the seeds.

   c Why are the seeds of legume plants so important for vegans?

8 Here are some common foods. Which parts of the plants do they come from?

   a Parsnip   **b** Broccoli   **c** Rhubarb   **d** Rice

   e Corn on the cob   **f** Potato   **g** Sprout

9 Write down two reasons why we don't eat all of the parts of a plant.

10 How is it possible to obtain energy for respiration from plants that we can't digest?

11 Here is a diagram of a path that a particular carbon atom has followed before it entered your body.

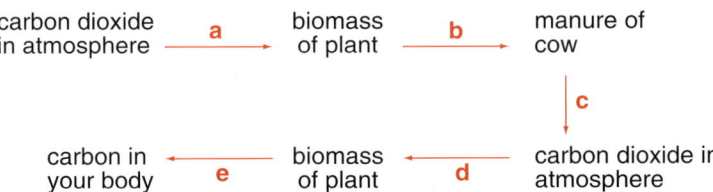

Each arrow indicates a particular process (such as combustion or photosynthesis) that results in the carbon atom moving from one location to another. Write down the process (or processes) that happens at each arrow.

12 Why are apples and pears sometimes called false fruits?

13 Pulses are high in protein because the plants that produce them are particularly good at obtaining nitrogen. How do they do this?

14 How are potatoes used to produce new plants?

How did I do?

	✔
I can state the parts of the plants that some common foods are obtained from.	☐
I can define what we mean by fruits, cereals and legumes and give an example of each.	☐
I can discuss the nutrients that can be obtained from common foods.	☐
I understand the different processes occurring in the carbon cycle.	☐

8: Improving the yield

You will revise:
- types of fertiliser and why they are needed
- herbicides and pesticides
- maximising photosynthesis.

Get started

In order to sustain an ever-growing human population, we need to make sure that we make food production as efficient as possible. Science can help us to find the best conditions for the plants that we grow for our food.

Practice

1 State three factors that control the rate of photosynthesis.

2 Why don't plants growing in natural habitats need fertilisers?

3 What is a biological pesticide?

4 Carefully describe what we mean by a weed.

Challenge

5 This question is about fertilisers.

   a Explain why farmers need to use fertilisers on their fields.

   b Manure is a good fertiliser. Where do the minerals in the manure originally come from?

   c State two advantages of using inorganic fertilisers rather than manure.

   d Ammonium nitrate is commonly used in fertilisers. Which element present in this compound is used by the plants?

   e Why is it important not to use too much fertiliser?

6 a Explain why weeds affect the yield of crops in a field.

   b What is the difference between a broad-spectrum and selective herbicide?

   c State one advantage and one disadvantage of using a broad-spectrum herbicide.

   d Spraying herbicide from the air enables you to cover a wide area of crops quickly. Explain one disadvantage of using this method.

   e What is a rather laborious alternative to using a weedkiller?

7 **a** State two ways in which insects can affect the crop yield.

b Explain, with reference to the food chain, why pesticides can adversely affect the local bird population.

c Some organic producers actually add insects to their greenhouses. How does this help the crops that they are growing?

8 **a** Explain why it is useful to find the conditions under which a crop has the greatest rate of photosynthesis.

Here are some graphs showing how the rate of photosynthesis is affected by light intensity, concentration of carbon dioxide and temperature.

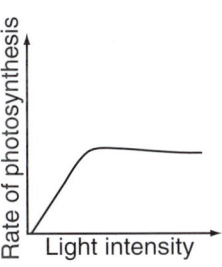
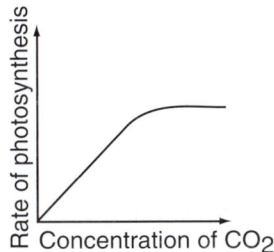
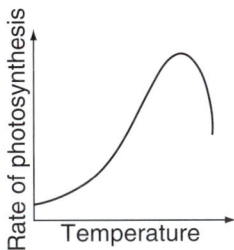

b When the data for the concentration of carbon dioxide graph was collected, how did the researcher ensure there was a fair test?

c Describe how the shape of the temperature graph differs from the other two.

d Why would commercial crop growers have to control the temperature of their greenhouses more carefully than the light intensity and the levels of carbon dioxide?

e Explain why the temperature would have no effect if the intensity of light is low.

9 Farmers often use polythene tunnels to grow their crops early in the season. Suggest two advantages of using these tunnels.

10 Greenhouses are naturally warmer than their outside surroundings. How do they work?

11 Why have fields increased in size in recent years?

12 Crop rotation is a way of keeping pests under control. How does it work? Why is it useful to have legume plants as one of the crops?

How did I do?

	✔
I can explain why we need to use fertilisers and discuss the advantages and disadvantages of the different types.	☐
I can describe the difference between herbicides and pesticides and the issues associated with their use.	☐
I can state three factors that affect the rate of photosynthesis and how these can be controlled.	☐

9: Metals and acids

You will revise:
- where metals are found on the periodic table
- the physical characteristics of metals
- the chemical reactions between metals and acids.

Get started

A very large proportion of the elements are metals. Most metals have similar physical properties but this family of elements can also be explored by studying the way they behave chemically. In particular, how do metals react with acids?

Practice

1 Where do metals appear on the periodic table?

2 Which metal is liquid at room temperature? Are any metals gases at this temperature?

3 Which metallic elements are magnetic?

4 Which gaseous element is usually produced when a metal reacts with an acid?

Challenge

5 **a** How do metals differ in appearance to non-metals (in the solid state)?

b The density of metals tends to be higher than the density of non-metals. Suggest how solid metals and non-metals differ in their structure.

c Metals can be polycrystalline. What does this mean?

d How do metals and non-metals differ in their ability to conduct heat?

e Do all metals conduct electricity equally well? What is special about graphite?

f State one advantage and one disadvantage of using metals as building materials.

6 Some sodium reacts with concentrated hydrochloric acid.

a Why would you be advised not to carry out this experiment in a school laboratory?

b What gas is produced from this reaction and how would you test for it?

c Once all of the sodium has reacted, how could you extract the solute from the solution?

d State the name of the solute that remains.

7 Here are formulae for some well-known chemicals:

Hydrogen gas: H_2
Hydrochloric acid: HCl
Sulfuric acid: H_2SO_4
Zinc sulfate: $ZnSO_4$
Zinc chloride: $ZnCl_2$

a Write down a balanced symbol equation for the reaction of zinc with

i sulfuric acid and   ii hydrochloric acid.

b What general name do we give to compounds like zinc sulfate and zinc chloride?

c Which other chemical is always present in these reactions?

d Suggest why this chemical plays a very important role in these reactions.

8 a What name do we call the compound K_2SO_4?

b Explain how you could obtain a sample of this substance from the reaction of a metal and an acid.

c Write down a balanced symbol equation for this reaction.

9 Copy and complete this word equation for the reaction between most metals and acids.

Metal + acid → . . . . . . + ...

10 CO_2 is called carbon dioxide. Why is $ZnCl_2$ called zinc chloride rather than zinc dichloride?

11 If you add 3 g of sodium to 200 ml of 0.5M sulfuric acid, the theoretical yield of sodium sulfate is 12.6 g.

a Suggest what is meant by theoretical yield.

b Explain why the mass of sodium sulfate produced is bigger than the original mass of the sodium.

c What would the theoretical yield be if you added 2 g of sodium to the same amount of sulfuric acid?

d Suggest why the theoretical yield is still 12.6 g when you add 5 g of sodium to the acid.

How did I do?

✔

I can identify metallic and non-metallic elements in the periodic table. ☐

I can describe the physical characteristics of metals. ☐

I can write a general word equation for the reaction between a metal and an acid. ☐

10: Other acidic reactions

You will revise:

You will revise:
- the definition of a salt
- reactions between metal carbonates and acids
- reactions between metal oxides and acids
- neutralisation reactions.

Get started

You have seen that metals tend to react with acids to produce a salt and hydrogen. Metal carbonates, metal oxides and alkalis react with acids in a particular way as well.

Practice

1 What do we mean by a metal oxide?

2 Outline the pH scale. Give some typical values for weak and strong acids and alkalis.

3 Some chemicals are used to work out the pH of a solution. What are these chemicals called?

4 Many chemical reactions produce heat energy. Where does this energy come from?

Challenge

5 This question is about the reaction between calcium carbonate and nitric acid.

a The chemical formula for calcium carbonate is $CaCO_3$. What percentage of the atoms in a calcium carbonate molecule are oxygen atoms?

b What percentage of the atoms in a calcium nitrate $Ca(NO_3)_2$ molecule are nitrogen atoms?

c The reaction produced bubbles of gas which turned limewater milky. What gas has been produced?

d What other indication might there be that a chemical reaction is happening?

e The calcium carbonate comes from marble chips. Outline briefly how marble is formed.

f Write a word equation for this reaction (there are three products including water).

g What would happen to the pH value of the solution as the reaction progressed?

6 **a** Write down the chemical formulae for **i** sulfuric acid, **ii** nitric acid and **iii** hydrochloric acid.

b State one similarity and one difference between these formulae.

c A salt is formed when a metal replaces the hydrogen in the acid. What three salts are formed when potassium replaces the hydrogen in sulfuric, nitric and hydrochloric acid?

d Do the sulfur and oxygen atoms often 'split up' from each other in reactions involving sulfuric acid? What does this tell you about the bonding between them?

7 Here is a symbol equation for a particular chemical reaction:

$$CuO + H_2SO_4 \rightarrow CuSO_4 + H_2O$$

a Write down the word equation for this reaction.

b Which compound in this reaction is a salt?

c This reaction happens quite slowly. Without changing the reactants in any way, how could you increase the rate of this reaction?

8 Here is a symbol equation for a particular neutralisation reaction:

$$Ca(OH)_2 + HNO_3 \rightarrow Ca(NO_3)_2 + H_2O$$

a Copy this equation and add numbers to make it properly balanced.

b Identify **i** the salt, **ii** the alkali and **iii** the acid in this reaction.

c If both reactants have completely reacted, what is the pH of the final solution?

9 Write the general word equations for:

a a metal carbonate reacting with an acid

b a metal oxide reacting with an acid

c an alkali reacting with an acid.

How did I do?

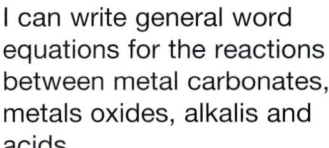

I can identify the salts in the reactions studied in this topic. ☐

I can write general word equations for the reactions between metal carbonates, metals oxides, alkalis and acids. ☐

I can predict how the pH value will change in these reactions. ☐

11: Reactivity of metals

You will revise:
- the reactivity series of metals
- the reactions of Group I and Group II metals with water
- other experimental methods for determining reactivity.

Get started

Some metals are more reactive than others. By studying chemical reactions we can place metals in a reactivity series. This helps us to predict what is going to happen in certain chemical reactions.

Practice

1. Explain why gold is found as an element in rocks rather than as a compound.

2. What is meant by the tarnishing of metals?

3. Suggest why the Bronze Age occurred before the Iron Age.

4. What chemical compound is rust? How does rust form? Why can it be a problem?

Challenge

5. Gold and sodium are both soft metals. When they are freshly cut, they are both shiny, but sodium quickly becomes dull in appearance. The gold, however, remains shiny.

   a Explain the difference in this behaviour.

   b Why do only the surfaces of metals become tarnished?

6. You have been given some magnesium, iron, copper and zinc and asked to determine their order of reactivity.

   To start with, you try placing the different metals in dilute hydrochloric acid. The magnesium reacted quickly, the zinc and the iron reacted quite slowly and the copper didn't react at all.

   a State two variables you need to control in order to make it a fair test.

   b Which two metals can you already place in the reactivity series?

   To test the reactivity of the other two metals you decide to collect the gas that they produce.

   c What is the gas produced? How could you test for it?

   d Suggest how you could determine which was the more reactive of these two metals.

7 The first three elements of Group I of the periodic table are lithium, sodium and potassium.

   a What are the chemical symbols for these three elements?

   b Summarise what you see when you place a small piece of each of these metals in water.

   c What gas is given off in these reactions? Why is this dangerous?

   d How could you show that the remaining solution is alkaline?

   e Write down these three elements in order of decreasing reactivity.

   f What are the metals further down this group? Why can't you see the reaction between these metals and water in a school lab?

   g Suggest why these three elements are highly flammable. Explain why it is inadvisable to put out a fire involving these metals with a water extinguisher.

   h Magnesium is a Group II metal that only reacts slowly with water. However, it does react with steam. State whether magnesium is more or less reactive than lithium.

   i Calcium, a Group II metal below magnesium in the periodic table, reacts fairly easily in cold water. Suggest how the reactivity of the Group II metals changes as you go down the group.

8 **a** What reaction is happening when you heat a metal in air?

   b Write a general equation for this reaction.

   c What does this suggest about the reactivity of the oxygen in the air compared to nitrogen or the noble gases?

   d Suggest what happens when you heat gold in air.

9 Suggest four properties of gold that make it suitable for extraction by 'panning' the sediment from streams. Explain your answer.

10 How can the reactivity series of metals be worked out using salt solutions and a voltmeter?

How did I do?

                                                   ✔

I can summarise the reactions of the Group I and Group II metals with water. ☐

I can determine the order of reactivity of metals from experimental results. ☐

I can use reactivity to explain why metals behave differently. ☐

12: Displacement reactions

You will revise:

- examples of displacement reactions
- using reactivity to determine the outcome of displacement reactions
- extraction of metals from metal ores
- the thermit reaction.

Get started

The reactivity series can be used to predict whether reactions take place. For example, a more reactive metal will displace a less reactive metal from a salt solution, but a less reactive metal won't be able to displace a more reactive metal.

Practice

1. What is a salt solution?

2. Explain what is meant by a displacement reaction.

3. Is the reaction between metals and acids a displacement reaction? Explain your answer.

4. Why are less reactive metals easier to extract from their ores than more reactive metals?

Challenge

5. Here is the reactivity series of some elements:

   K, Na, Ca, Mg, Al, C, Zn, Fe, Pb, H, Cu, Au

   a Write out the names of these elements.

   b Does the order of increasing reactivity go left or right along this list?

   c Which elements in this list are non-metals?

   d What element could you use to displace sodium from common salt?

   e Which two elements wouldn't react with dilute hydrochloric acid? Explain your answer.

6. Coke is often used to extract metals from metal ores.

   a What do we mean by a metal ore?

   b Coke is formed when coal is heated without air to remove unwanted tars and gas. Why mustn't there be any air?

   c Which element from the list in question 5 is coke made from?

   d Iron is obtained from iron oxide in the Earth's crust. Suggest, very simply, how coke can be used to remove the iron from the iron oxide.

e Why would this method not be possible for the extraction of calcium?

7 a Compounds formed from the most reactive metals are said to be very stable. Explain why this is the case.

b Suggest how the amount of heat given out when a compound is formed depends on the stability of the compound.

8 a If an iron nail is placed in copper sulfate solution, the nail turns from grey to brown and the solution turns from blue to green. Explain what is happening.

b Magnesium sulfate is colourless. What would happen if you placed an iron nail in magnesium sulfate?

c What would happen if you placed magnesium in iron sulfate?

9 The thermit reaction is a reaction between aluminium and iron oxide.

a Write down a word equation for this reaction.

b Two of the compounds involved are Fe_2O_3 and Al_2O_3. Use this information to write a balanced symbol equation.

c Explain why the reaction is more vigorous if the reactants are in powdered form and they are mixed well together in the right proportions.

d How is the reaction started?

e Once the reaction has started it gives out a lot of heat. Explain how this is useful for joining railway tracks.

f Explain why you couldn't use copper instead of aluminium. Why couldn't you use potassium?

10 Even though carbon isn't very far up the reactivity series, why is coke used a lot in commercial extraction?

11 Apart from preserving iron resources, why is it important to recycle as much iron as possible?

12 Aluminium and iron are both materials used to build cars. Aluminium is more reactive than iron. Why is the reaction between iron and the oxygen in the air much more of a problem than the reaction between aluminium and oxygen?

13 The more reactive metals cannot be displaced from their compounds very easily using chemical methods. However, many can be extracted using electrolysis. How does electrolysis work? What role does water play?

How did I do?

I can complete a word equation illustrating a displacement reaction. ☐

I can use the reactivity series to determine whether a particular metal is going to react with a given salt solution. ☐

When presented with a method of extracting a metal from a metal ore, I can explain the reactions that take place. ☐

I can describe the thermit reaction and how it is used. ☐

13: Acidity in the environment

You will revise:
- what we mean by acid rain
- natural and human causes of acid rain
- the harmful effects of acid rain on the environment.

Get started

Rain is naturally slightly acidic. However, the activity of humans has sometimes increased this acidity, causing damage to the environment.

Practice

1 Carefully define what we mean by acid rain.

2 Explain what is meant by the weathering of rocks.

3 How does weathering lead to the formation of soils?

4 Why do you find many more lichens on trees in the countryside than you do in a city?

Challenge

5 **a** Carbon dioxide, sulfur dioxide and nitrogen dioxide all dissolve in water to form different types of acid. Write down an acid that is formed from each of these compounds.

b Give an example of the natural production of carbon dioxide.

c Why is the rain particularly acidic following a volcanic eruption?

6 Car exhausts emit nitrogen monoxide which can lead to acid rain. In recent years all new cars have been fitted with catalytic converters. The following reaction occurs inside the converters:

$$2CO + 2NO \rightarrow 2CO_2 + N_2$$

a What other harmful gas does the catalytic converter remove from the exhaust fumes?

b Explain why, even if all of the nitrogen monoxide is removed, car exhausts still lead to acid rain.

c What conclusion can you reach about the acidity of nitric acid and carbonic acid?

7 **a** What is the difference between erosion and corrosion?

b Why is limestone particularly susceptible to acid rain?

c Explain why acid rain could be particularly damaging in big cities in hot climates.

d Iron railings can gradually get thinner due to the action of acid rain. Would this also happen with gold railings? Explain your answer.

8 **a** Acid rain can dissolve minerals in the soil, which can then flow away with the rainwater. Explain why this is a major problem for plants.

b Acid rain can also directly damage plants. Explain why acidic mist is likely to be even more damaging.

c In Sweden, lakes are sprayed with limestone every few years. How does the limestone reduce the effect of acid rain? Why does the process have to be repeated?

9 Here is a diagram showing a cross-section of some soil.

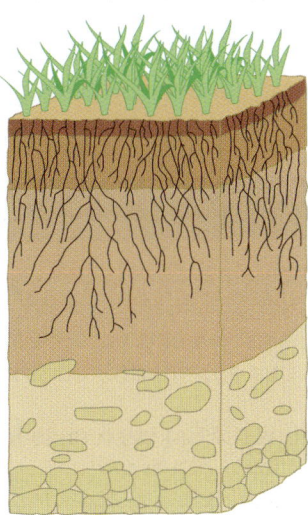

a What is the main cause of the weathering of the rocks at the bottom of the soil?

b Besides the minerals from the rocks, how do the other minerals get into the soil (assuming no human intervention)?

c In Scandinavian countries, the soil is coarse textured, allowing water to move easily. Some base minerals form alkaline solutions in the water. Explain why the soil is often very acidic.

10 Why are scientists investigating the use of limestone-secreting bacteria in preservation work?

11 State and explain three factors that can affect the pH of natural soil.

12 Why is acid rain becoming less of a problem than it was a generation ago?

How did I do?

I can explain how acid rain is produced naturally. ☐

I can discuss how human activities are leading to increased levels of acid rain. ☐

I can describe what effects these increased levels are having on the environment. ☐

14: Air pollution and global warming

You will revise:

- various ways in which humans are polluting the atmosphere
- greenhouse gases and global warming
- possible impacts of global warming
- ways in which we can reduce air pollution.

Get started

Human life since the Industrial Revolution has become much easier but our activities have caused damage to the environment. Can we solve the problem of air pollution or have we left a legacy for hundreds of years to come?

Practice

1 State a reason why air pollution has become more of a problem in the last few hundred years.

2 What is the difference between global warming and climate change?

3 Why is carbon dioxide called a greenhouse gas?

4 Besides polluting the atmosphere, what is the main problem of using fossil fuels as an energy resource?

Challenge

5 a What chemical element is present in ozone?

   b The ozone layer is high up in the atmosphere and absorbs a lot of ultraviolet light from the Sun. Why is this essential for our survival?

   c Why has the use of chlorofluorocarbons (CFCs) been phased out in recent years?

   d Give one example where CFCs have been used in the past.

   e Why will it take a very long time for this ban to have a sizeable effect on the environment?

6 When the fuel in a car engine doesn't burn efficiently, carbon monoxide is formed.

   a What is the chemical formula for carbon monoxide?

   b Carbon monoxide atoms readily attach themselves to haemoglobin in the blood. Why is carbon monoxide such a dangerous gas?

   c Why can carbon monoxide poisoning due to a faulty gas boiler catch you unawares?

7 What is smog? Why is it less likely to occur in big cities than it did in the 1950s?

8　**a** Explain why most factories and power stations have very tall chimneys.

　　b Does this ultimately solve the pollution problem?

　　c When particles of soot pass electrical wires at very high negative voltage they become negatively charged. Explain how the presence of positively charged plates within a chimney can extract the soot from the exhaust gases.

9　**a** What is biodegradable waste?

　　b Explain why biodegradable waste is less harmful to the environment.

10　**a** Explain how the presence of carbon dioxide (and other greenhouse gases) in the atmosphere leads to the surface of the Earth being hotter than it would have been.

　　b Did the greenhouse effect happen before humans polluted the atmosphere?

　　c How do we know that levels of carbon dioxide have risen dramatically since the 1950s?

　　d Give two reasons why global warming will lead to higher sea levels.

　　e Researchers can find information about the carbon dioxide content of the atmosphere and the temperature of the climate from millions of years ago by drilling deep into the ice in Antarctica. Why is this data useful in helping us to predict what is going to happen in the future?

　　f Most scientists agree that the Earth's average temperature rose by 0.6 °C in the 20th century. Why was this measurement very difficult to make?

11 Will the melting of icebergs lead to a rise in sea levels? Do an experiment with an ice cube floating in some water to find out. Try to explain what is going on.

12 State two other factors that might be the reason for global warming other than increased carbon dioxide levels.

13 Some people have suggested that climate change could disrupt the Gulf Stream. What is the Gulf Stream? What impact would it have on the UK climate if it stopped?

14 Scientists have concluded that spring in the UK is getting slightly earlier every year. Why can plants adapt to the changing climate faster than animals? What impact could this have on bird life and animals further up the food chain?

How did I do?

I can explain why there is a hole in the ozone layer and why this is bad news. ☐

I can describe what we mean by smog and ways in which we can reduce it appearing. ☐

I can discuss the likely impact of increased carbon dioxide emissions on the environment. ☐

15: Chemical energy

You will revise:

◗ the relationship between chemical energy and atomic bonds

◗ exothermic and endothermic reactions

◗ activation energy.

Get started

In some reactions, chemical energy is transformed into heat energy and the temperature increases. In other reactions the opposite happens. It's all to do with the chemical bonds.

Practice

1 What is the general name for **a** reactions that emit heat energy and **b** reactions that absorb heat energy?

2 When a liquid freezes into a solid, is heat energy given out or is heat energy needed?

3 What is happening to the bonds when a liquid freezes?

4 Write down a general rule about whether heat energy is absorbed or emitted when bonds are made or broken.

Challenge

5 Explain why steam at 100 °C can burn you more than the same amount of boiling water.

6 Hydrogen produces a lot of heat when it burns in oxygen to form water.

　a Write down a balanced symbol equation for this reaction.

　b State and explain two problems of using hydrogen as a fuel.

　c People have called hydrogen a clean fuel. Why can hydrogen be considered in this way?

7 **a** What is the relationship between the reactivity of a particular metal and the strength of bonds it forms in its compounds?

　b If you wanted to obtain as much energy as possible from a displacement reaction, what sort of materials would you choose?

　c Although the thermit reaction (between iron oxide and aluminium) produces a lot of heat, why do you need to start it off by supplying heat (e.g. with a magnesium fuse)? Explain your answer by referring to the chemical bonds involved.

8 By considering the movement of the particles, suggest why reactions happen at a higher rate at higher temperatures.

9 Here is an equation involving methane:

$$CH_4 + 2O_2 \rightarrow 2H_2O + CO_2$$

a What type of reaction is this?

b Why do bonds have to be broken for this reaction to happen?

c Explain why you need to supply heat energy to start the reaction.

d Once the reaction has started, it produces a lot of heat. Where does this extra heat come from?

Sometimes methane can react with oxygen in the following way:

$$3CH_4 + 4O_2 \rightarrow 6H_2O + 2CO + C$$

e Show that this reaction is balanced properly.

f Compare the ratio of methane to oxygen in the two reactions.

g Suggest under what conditions methane reacts with oxygen using the second equation.

h What is the difference between CO and Co?

i Explain a cause of soot in the smoke produced while burning natural gas.

10 a Write down the word equations for respiration and photosynthesis.

b Respiration releases chemical energy. Why must this mean that photosynthesis requires energy?

c The energy produced by the Sun would not normally be enough to power photosynthesis. How do plants and some bacteria get over this problem?

11 Sometimes you can use the energy from chemical reactions to provide electrical energy.

a A cell using zinc and copper electrodes produces a voltage of 1.10 V, whereas a cell using iron and copper electrodes produces a voltage of 0.78 V. Assuming that this is a fair test, which is the more reactive, zinc or iron?

b Suggest what voltage a cell using zinc and iron electrodes would produce.

How did I do?

I can explain where the extra heat energy in an exothermic reaction comes from. ☐

I know why energy is needed to start a chemical reaction. ☐

I can describe the role of enzymes and catalysts in terms of reducing the energy needed for a reaction. ☐

16: Making new materials

Get started

All chemical processes involve breaking and making atomic bonds. No matter is created or destroyed so the mass always stays the same. However, a simple rearranging of bonds can create a wealth of new materials with useful physical and chemical properties.

Practice

1. What is the difference between a physical and a chemical property?

2. Mono-, di-, -ate and poly- are all prefixes or suffixes commonly used to describe chemicals. Describe the meaning of each one.

3. a What are the chemical formulae for **i** sulfur trioxide, **ii** hydrogen peroxide (water with an extra oxygen atom)?

   b Suggest why hydrogen peroxide is often called an oxidising agent.

Challenge

4. Antoine Lavoisier discovered that mass was conserved in all chemical reactions and so he overturned the phlogiston theory.

   a What is meant by the conservation of mass?

   b The phlogiston theory explains that objects burn by allowing a substance (phlogiston) to escape which is the source of the heat. How would the mass of burning objects change according to this theory?

   c Drilling a hole into some wood produces heat. **i** Describe how the phlogiston theory explains this phenomenon. **ii** How would today's science explain what is happening?

   d Joseph Priestly discovered a gas in which objects burned more brightly. Why did he call this gas 'dephlogisticated air'?

   e What gas was Priestly actually using?

   f Lavoisier explained why the mass of burning objects can increase. How does modern science explain this phenomenon?

5. a Where do the atoms in our bodies originally come from?

   b What happens to our atoms when we die?

   c Explain how none of this could happen if there was no energy from the Sun.

6 If mass is conserved in all reactions, where does the mass of a burning candle go?

7 **a** 2.4 g of magnesium was burned in some oxygen. The resulting magnesium oxide had a mass of 4.0 g. What mass of oxygen reacted with the magnesium?

b There are the same numbers of magnesium atoms as oxygen atoms in magnesium oxide. Why was your answer to part **a** not 2.4 g?

c What mass of magnesium oxide would you expect when you burn 3.2 g of magnesium?

8 **a** Amino acids are used to make proteins. Explain why there is an endless variety of proteins even though there are only about 20 different amino acids.

b What is the relationship between DNA, amino acids and proteins?

c Silk is a particular form of protein obtained from the cocoons of silkworms. Suggest why it is difficult to obtain in large quantities.

d In 1931 Wallace Carothers discovered how to produce nylon – a fibre with similar properties to silk – from simple chemical reactions. Explain why some items of clothing became much cheaper.

e Just before the Second World War, rubber was an essential material. It was produced in only a few far-eastern countries. Why was it important for chemists in western countries to try to develop a synthetic chemical with similar properties?

9 This diagram shows a molecule of ethene and a molecule of polythene.

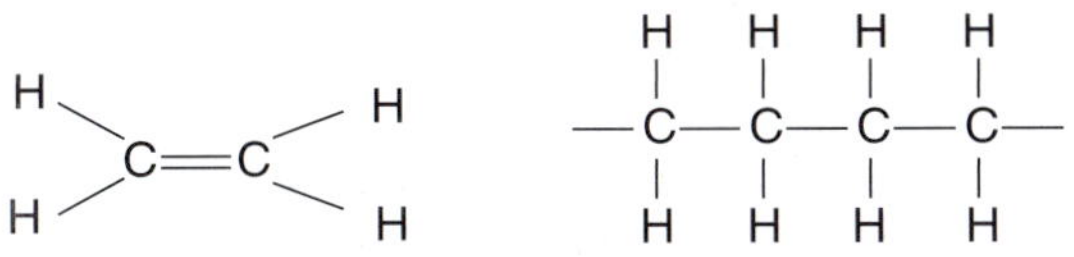

Ethene   Polythene

a What does the double line mean between the carbon atoms in the ethene molecule?

b The polythene molecule is drawn with lines to the left and the right. Suggest what this means about the length of the molecule.

c Carbon atoms like to make four bonds. Describe simply how lots of ethene molecules can be combined to form a polythene molecule.

d State one use of polythene.

How did I do?

I can explain why mass must be conserved in all chemical reactions. ☐

I can describe the phlogiston theory and how modern science has overturned these ideas. ☐

I can appreciate that modern materials are made from existing chemicals but with the atoms rearranged in different ways. ☐

17: Energy and electricity

You will revise:

▶ energy transformations in an electric circuit

▶ using voltmeters and ammeters to measure voltage and current

▶ studying energy transformations by measuring the voltage.

Get started

Electric circuits involve energy being transformed from one form to another. You can examine how the energy changes by considering the voltage between various points in the circuit.

Practice

1 What energy transformation happens inside a cell?

2 How do you connect ammeters and voltmeters in a circuit?

3 What is the voltage between two points in a circuit actually a measure of?

4 Explain the difference between an energy transformation and an energy transfer.

Challenge

5 What useful energy transformations happen in the following devices?

    a Electric motor   **b** Microphone

    c Variable resistor   **d** Solar cell

6 **a** Explain the principle of conservation of energy.

    b When we burn fossil fuels, where does the wasted energy go?

7 Here are some diagrams showing how two light bulbs transform the energy.

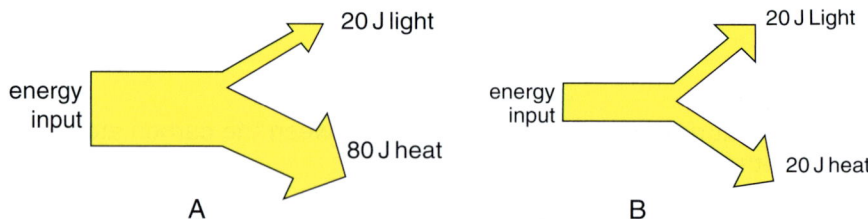

    A   B

    a How much energy has each light bulb used?

    b Which light bulb is the most efficient? Explain your answer.

8 This diagram shows a circuit with various places where a voltmeter can be connected.

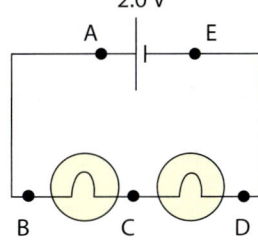

a Explain, in terms of electrical charges, what we mean by a current.

b If the connecting wires behave perfectly, how much electrical energy is transformed into other forms of energy between points A and B?

c What value would a voltmeter display if it was connected to A and B?

d Copy and complete the following table (assume the light bulbs are identical).

Places where voltmeter is connected	Voltmeter reading
A and E	i
B and D	ii
B and C	iii
C and D	iv
D and E	v

e Another identical light bulb is added in series to the circuit. What would the voltmeter read if it was connected across i one light bulb, ii two light bulbs?

9 You can make a cell to power an electrical clock by placing copper and magnesium electrodes in a potato.

a Where does the energy which powers the clock come from?

b Why does the cell run out?

c Explain why the cell wouldn't work if you used two copper electrodes instead.

d Potassium is a more reactive metal than magnesium and would produce a higher voltage. Why would it be difficult to use a potassium electrode?

10 The proper term for voltage is *potential difference*. Explain why this term is used. Assuming each charge carrier has an electrical potential energy of 2 J as it emerges from the positive terminal, how does the energy of the charge carriers vary as they move around the circuit (starting at A) in question **8**?

How did I do?

	✔
I can describe the energy transformations occurring in a particular electric circuit.	☐
I can connect ammeters and voltmeters to measure current and voltage.	☐
I can explain how voltages vary across components in a circuit in terms of energy transformations.	☐

18: Electricity and modern life

You will revise:
- why electricity is so useful
- how electricity is produced
- the relationship between energy and power
- calculating electricity costs.

Get started

It is difficult to overestimate the impact that electricity has had on modern life. However, if we are to keep the costs down and have a sustainable future, we must use it efficiently.

Practice

1 What happens to the size of the current as it flows through a series circuit?

2 State one advantage and one disadvantage of using mains electricity rather than batteries.

3 What is the voltage of mains electricity in houses in the UK?

4 When would you use a 10 W light bulb instead of a 100 W light bulb (assuming they have the same efficiency)?

Challenge

5 **a** Why do we sometimes call electricity a secondary fuel?

   b By considering the energy transformations in useful devices around the home, explain why electricity is a very useful source of energy.

   c State one other reason why electricity is a useful resource.

6 **a** The total current entering a house is 60 A. Under normal operating conditions, what value would the current leaving the house be?

   b Why would there be cause for concern if the current leaving the house was at a smaller value than this?

   c Are the mains sockets in buildings connected in series or parallel? Explain your answer.

   d When there is a larger current flowing into the house, the electricity meter 'counts up' at a faster rate. What quantity is it measuring?

7 The amount of electrical energy you use is charged in kilowatt-hours (or units). Here is the formula to work it out:

   energy (in kW h) = power (in kW) × time (in hours).

a If the electricity company charge 10p per kilowatt-hour, how much does it cost to watch a 0.5 kW TV for 8 hours?

b How many units are used when a 100 W light bulb is switched on for 20 minutes? (1 kW = 1000 W)

8 A teacher set up the following apparatus

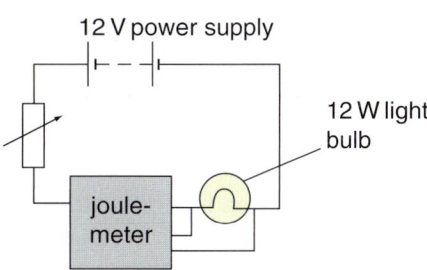

12 V power supply

12 W light bulb

joule-meter

a The joulemeter clicked every time the light bulb transformed 10 J of energy. What energy transformations are taking place?

b What did pupils hear when the teacher adjusted the variable resistor to make the light bulb brighter?

c The teacher took out the 12 W light bulb and replaced it with a 24 W bulb. The variable resistor was not changed. What did the pupils see and hear that was different?

d What is the relationship between power and energy?

e What would happen if the teacher replaced the 24 W bulb with a more efficient bulb of the same brightness?

9 Here is a diagram of a simple dynamo.

a What energy transformation takes place inside the dynamo?

b Why is the coil wound on a piece of iron?

c State three things you could do to make the current larger.

ridged wheel driven by tyre

cylindrical magnet

coil of wire wound on iron

current to lamps

10 Why do electricity companies have to follow the TV schedules very closely?

11 Explain why electricity is transmitted along power lines at such a high voltage. Why don't birds sitting on the lines get an electric shock?

How did I do?

I can give two reasons why electricity is very useful. ☐

I can state how the power of a light bulb is related to the energy it uses. ☐

I can calculate the electrical energy used in kWh and how much it will cost. ☐

19: Gravity and orbits

You will revise:
- the difference between mass and weight
- how forces affect motion
- why gravity makes objects orbit more massive objects.

Get started

The force of gravity is an attractive force between all masses. The size of the force depends on the amount of mass and the distance. Gravity can make objects in space orbit more massive objects.

Practice

1 What is the definition of an object's weight?

2 How does this differ from an object's mass?

3 If the Sun's gravity suddenly disappeared, what would be the motion of the Earth?

4 Why do we feel the gravity from the Earth much more than the gravity from the Sun?

Challenge

5 **a** If the Earth pulls with a force of 10 N on every kg mass on its surface. What is the weight of **i** 60 kg, **ii** 500 g?

b What mass has a weight of **i** 50 N, **ii** 1 N on the Earth?

6 **a** Give one reason why the pull of the Moon's gravity on objects at its surface is one-sixth as much as the Earth's.

b What is the weight of a 60 kg object on the Moon?

c What mass has a weight of 12 N on the Moon?

7 A spaceship has a weight of 2400 N on the Moon. It then goes to a planet where it has a weight of 32 000 N.

Find **a** the mass of the spaceship and **b** the force with which gravity pulls on 1 kg of matter on the planet.

8 **a** Which way does the Sun's gravity pull you at noon?

b If you dug down to the centre of the Earth (and survived), what would you notice about the gravity acting on you?

c Explain why the Moon orbits the Earth rather than the Sun even though the Sun has a larger mass.

9 **a** A rocket has a weight of 10 000 N. Explain why the rocket motor has to provide a force greater than 10 000 N in order to accelerate the rocket upwards.

b Once the rocket has taken off its acceleration increases although the rocket motor is providing the same force. Suggest two reasons why the acceleration increases.

c The rocket reaches deep outer space and the rocket motors are switched off. What is the motion of the rocket now?

10 You are whirling a conker above your head in a horizontal circle.

a What direction must the force act on the conker to keep it moving in a circle?

b What would happen to the conker if you let go of the string?

c When a car goes around a roundabout, what provides the force that makes it go in a circle? What might happen if there is ice on the road?

11 Here is a diagram of the path that a rock would follow if you threw it sideways while standing on a chair.

a What is making the rock fall to the ground? Which direction does this force act?

b Why doesn't the rock simply fall vertically?

c Copy the diagram and include the path the rock would follow if you threw it faster.

d If you throw the rock at about 7 km/s it falls at the same rate as the Earth curves away. What would the rock do if there are no obstructions (and there was no air resistance)?

e Why don't objects need to be as fast as this to behave in the same way if they are further away from the Earth?

12 The Earth actually bulges at the equator due to its rotation. How does your weight vary between the equator and the North Pole? Explain your answer.

13 You dig a tunnel downwards to the centre of the Earth and then all the way to the other side of the Earth. You then stand on the surface of the Earth by the opening of the tunnel and jump into the tunnel. What would your motion be?

How did I do?

I can calculate the weight of an object on Earth if I know its mass. ☐

I can do calculations based on masses and weights of objects if they are on the Moon or other planets. ☐

I can describe the motion of an object if there is an unbalanced force on it. ☐

I can explain how gravity can make objects move in circular orbits. ☐

20: Understanding the Solar System

You will revise:

- how our understanding of the Solar System has changed
- the scientific evidence that led to our changing ideas
- the orbits and uses of artificial satellites.

Get started

Early models of the Solar System lasted for a very long time before observations and new scientific theories forced people to accept that these models were wrong. In recent years our understanding of the Solar System has quickly improved due to the use of artificial satellites and space probes.

Practice

1. Before the seventeenth century, which object did most people think was at the centre of the Solar System?

2. What invention led to the realisation that the Sun was at the centre of the Solar System?

3. Why did it take many years for most people in western civilisations to accept that this was indeed the case?

4. What is the benefit of having a telescope up in space?

Challenge

5. This question is about artificial satellites.

   a What is a geostationary (or geosynchronous) orbit?

   b What are satellites in geostationary orbits generally used for? What is the advantage of this particular type of orbit?

   c What is a polar orbit?

   d Polar orbits are much nearer to the Earth than geostationary orbits. Explain why this means that they must orbit the Earth much more quickly.

   e Explain how satellites in polar orbits can photograph most of the Earth's surface over a period of 24 hours.

   f State two uses of polar satellites.

   g Draw a diagram of the Earth and the orbits of a geostationary and a polar satellite.

   h What are satellites orbiting other planets used for?

6

a What is the evidence in the night sky that the Earth is spinning?

b If you didn't know that the Earth was spinning, what other conclusion could you reach about the motion of the stars?

c To the unaided eye, the visible planets look just like stars. Where does the light from the planets ultimately come from?

d How did astronomers know that the planets were different to the stars before the telescope was invented?

7 In AD 140 Ptolemy produced a model of the Universe that fitted the known facts of the time.

a Why was it important that the model fitted the known facts?

b Astronomers noticed that the planets other than Mercury and Venus spent some of their orbits (around the Earth remember) going backwards. How did Ptolemy adapt his model to account for this motion?

c As time went on and astronomers made better measurements, the model had to be continually altered. Why was this?

d In 1543 Copernicus suggested that a model of the Universe with the Sun at its centre fitted the facts just as well and was a lot simpler. Why was he largely ignored?

8

a How did Galileo's telescopic observations of Jupiter prove that not everything orbited the Earth?

b People originally believed that gravity was due to objects trying to get to the centre of the Universe. Why was this 'evidence' for Ptolemy's Earth-centred model?

c What role did Newton play in leading most people to accept the fact that the Sun was at the centre of the Universe?

9 We now know that the Sun is not at the centre of the Universe. Briefly describe our understanding of the structure of the Universe today.

10 There has been much debate recently about whether Pluto should be called a planet. What discoveries have led to this debate?

11 Newton's theory of gravity led to the discovery of a new planet. How did this come about? Why did this add weight to the evidence that his theory was correct?

12 What sort of object do we think we are orbiting at the centre of the Milky Way galaxy? What is the evidence for this?

How did I do?

✔

I can outline the evidence that led to us realising that the Sun was at the centre of the Solar System rather than the Earth. ☐

I can discuss why these changing ideas met a lot of resistance. ☐

I can draw diagrams of geostationary and polar orbits and explain the uses of satellites that travel in these orbits. ☐

21: Speed, distance and time

You will revise:

- the formula linking average speed, distance and time
- converting the units for speed
- calculating speeds, distances and times
- measuring the speed at a point.

Get started

The average speed of a car journey is the distance travelled divided by the time taken. However, the speed often changes, from accelerating up to high speed on a motorway to slowing to a stop at some traffic lights. How can speed be measured more precisely and how can it be measured at a point?

Practice

1. Write down the formula that links average speed, distance and time.

2. A car goes a certain distance in a certain time. If another car goes half the distance in a third of the time, is its average speed faster or slower?

3. How many metres are there in a kilometre? How many seconds are there in an hour?

4. The Earth orbits the Sun at a speed of 30 km/s. What is this speed in km/h?

5. If a jet aeroplane is travelling at 1200 km/h, how far does it travel per second?

Challenge

6. Convert the following speeds into different units:

   a 36 km/h into m/h   d 72 m/s into km/h

   b 36 km/h into m/s   e 144 km/h into m/s

   c 200 m/s into km/s   f 20 m/s into km/h

7. Two bikes are racing down a hill. The first bike is going at a constant speed of 10 m/s and the second bike is gradually accelerating from rest. Both bikes start at the top and arrive at the bottom of the hill together.

   a What is the average speed of the second bike?

   b Which bike was in front at the halfway point?

8. I walk to my friend's house, which is 6 km away. At exactly the moment I leave my house, my friend leaves her house and walks towards me. If I am walking twice as fast as my friend, how far away from my house do we meet?

9 A teacher is timing the winning time of a school 100 m race. After the starting pistol has been fired, he fumbles a little before he manages to start the stopwatch. If the average speed was calculated from this time, would it be too fast or too slow?

10 A teacher sets up an air track with two light gates connected to a datalogger. The card on the 'glider' that breaks the beam of the light gates is 2 cm long. The datalogger is set up to read the times that the beams of light have been broken. When the glider was sent along the air track, the first light gate read a time of 0.102 s and the second light gate read a time of 0.051 s.

    a Was the glider speeding up or slowing down?

    b Calculate the speeds in cm/s at the two light gates.

    c Would it be possible to work out the average speed of the glider from the data you have been given? Explain your answer.

    d Can the light gates give you the actual speed the glider was travelling as it went past them or is this still an average speed?

11 Here is a diagram showing the basic parts of a speedometer in a car.

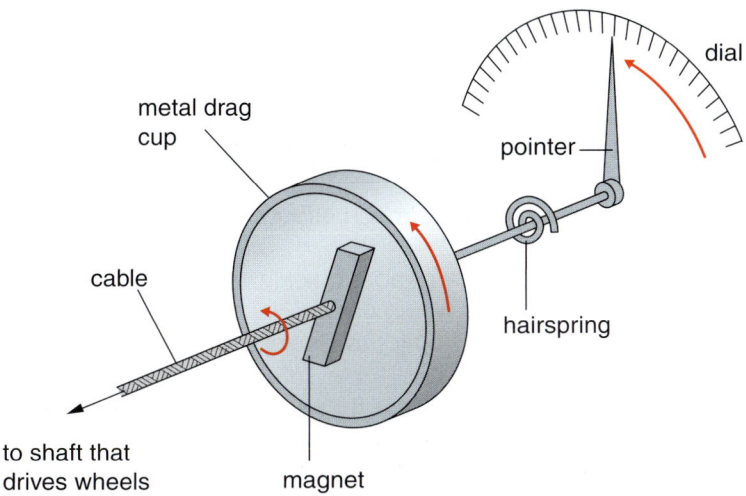

    a As the magnet turns, it exerts a force on the metal drag cup. Explain how the rest of the speedometer works.

    b Does the speedometer measure an average speed or does it measure the speed at a point? Explain your answer.

How did I do?

	✔
I can calculate the average speed from the distance and the time.	☐
I can convert speeds between m/s and km/h.	☐
I can analyse different motions and carry out calculations based on them.	☐
I can describe how a speedometer works.	☐

22: Forces and motion

You will revise:

- the motion of objects when the forces are balanced or unbalanced
- how the force of air resistance changes with speed
- terminal velocity and why things have a maximum speed.

Get started

When the forces are balanced, an object will maintain its present speed. However, unbalanced forces make the object speed up, slow down or change direction.

Practice

1. The right-hand pedal in a car changes the force provided by the engine. Why is it called an accelerator?

2. How does the maximum acceleration of a car change when it is fully loaded?

3. How does the air feel different when you are riding a bicycle quickly? How do you reduce this effect?

4. What is terminal velocity?

5. Explain the difference between upthrust and air resistance.

Challenge

6. When you stop pedalling on a bicycle and freewheel you will gradually slow down.

   a What is the main force that makes you slow down to start with?

   b Why doesn't this force have much effect when you are going slowly?

   c Explain why you slow down more quickly when you apply the brakes.

   d Why do you skid if you apply the brakes too quickly?

7. Many car manufacturers give the time it takes for a car to get from 0 to 60 mph.

   a If a car can get from 0 to 60 mph in 4.8 s is its acceleration more or less than a car that can get from 0 to 60 mph in 10 s?

   b State and explain three factors that car manufacturers can change in their cars to improve these times.

   c Why do cars have a maximum speed rather than just being able to accelerate for ever?

   d Does the mass of a car affect its maximum speed? Explain your answer.

8 Here is a speed–time graph of a scrunched-up piece of paper falling through the air.

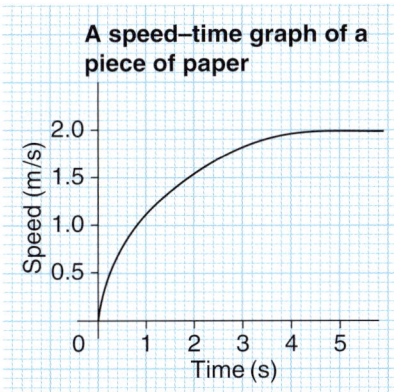

A speed–time graph of a piece of paper

a Describe the motion shown by the graph.

b State the two forces acting on the piece of paper and the direction they are acting in.

c How does the size of each of these forces depend on the speed of the paper?

d As the paper gets faster, why does the resultant force downwards get less?

e What happens to the forces when the paper reaches its terminal velocity?

f How many seconds into the journey did the paper reach its terminal velocity? What is the value of this velocity?

g How would the shape of the graph differ if **i** the paper was shaped into a parachute, **ii** the paper was shaped into a dart that pointed vertically downwards?

9 **a** A space capsule slows down as it enters the atmosphere. What does this mean about the size of the air resistance compared to the capsule's weight?

b What happens to the sizes of the forces as the capsule slows down? Why does it reach a terminal velocity?

c What piece of equipment can the capsule use to reduce its terminal velocity to a safe level for touchdown?

d Why couldn't this equipment be used as the capsule first entered the atmosphere?

23: Pressure

You will revise:
- calculating pressures
- pressures in gases
- using hydraulic machines.

Get started

The pressure produced by a force depends on the area of the surface the force is acting on. By understanding pressure, we can design machines to make our lives easier.

Practice

1. Write down the formula relating pressure, force and surface area.

2. The force has to be perpendicular to the surface area. What does perpendicular mean?

3. Why do your ears hurt more and more when you dive deeper into water?

4. What is the difference between a hydraulic and a pneumatic system?

Challenge

5. A 1 kg rectangular block (with weight 10 N) measuring 2 cm by 1 cm by 4 cm is placed on a table.

   a What is the largest pressure the block can exert on the table?

   b What is the least pressure?

6. Give an example in nature where an animal's body has been designed to produce as much pressure as possible and another example where part of the body has been designed to produce as little pressure as possible.

7. Here is a simple hydraulic jack.

   a Why wouldn't the jack work very well using air instead of liquid?

   b What pressure is in the liquid?

   c What load is the 2 N force managing to lift?

   d By how much does the jack multiply the forces?

8 To make sure that a vehicle is safe, you need to check the air pressure in the tyres.

    a Why are pressures that are too high or low, unsafe?

    b Explain why lorries have four (or more) wheels parallel to each other on a given axle, rather than just two wheels like a car.

    c When roads are covered in snow, why does it sometimes help to let down your tyres?

    d Tractor wheels have a very large radius and their tyres are very wide. Explain why this is useful.

9 The diagram below shows air in a gas syringe and air in a fixed container. The air is then heated.

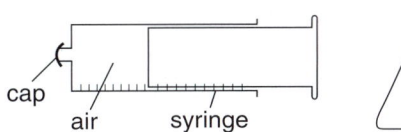 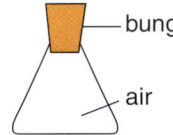

    a In which piece of apparatus will the volume change and the pressure stay the same?

    b What happens to the pressure and volume in the other piece of apparatus?

10 This diagram is of a water-filled balloon pierced with holes. State two pieces of information about the pressure in liquids you can work out from the diagram.

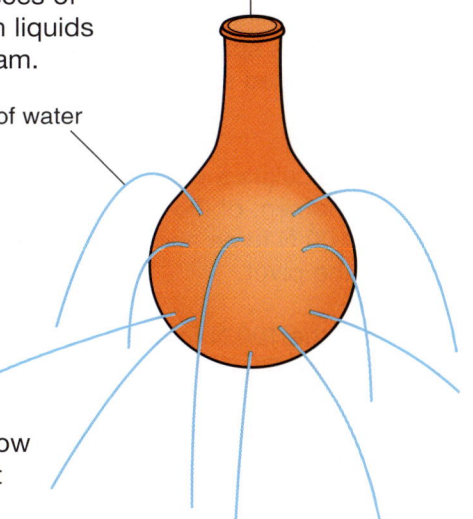

water-filled balloon

jets of water

11 **a** If something is fully submerged in some water (but not touching the bottom), which direction does the water pressure act on
i the bottom, **ii** the top of the object?

    b By considering how pressure changes with depth, explain how fluids can produce an upthrust force.

24: Levers and moments

You will revise:
- calculating the moment of a force
- using moments to study how forces can balance see-saws
- explaining how levers work.

Get started

Levers can be used to multiply forces or distances. A force acting on a lever can produce a turning effect called a moment. By studying moments you can explain how objects can balance and the size of forces needed to make them balance.

Practice

1 What is the moment of a force?

2 Explain the principle of moments and when it can be applied.

3 Why are door handles placed far away from the hinge?

4 In what way does a steering wheel act like a lever?

Challenge

5 If a 200 g mass is placed 15 cm away from a fulcrum on a see-saw, how far away from the fulcrum must you place a 150 g mass to make the see-saw balance?

6 Would your answer to question **5** be the same on the Moon, even though the weights would be different? Explain your answer.

7 Explain why the lowest gear on your bike is easy to pedal, but the top gear requires much more force.

8 Here is a spanner being used to tighten a nut.

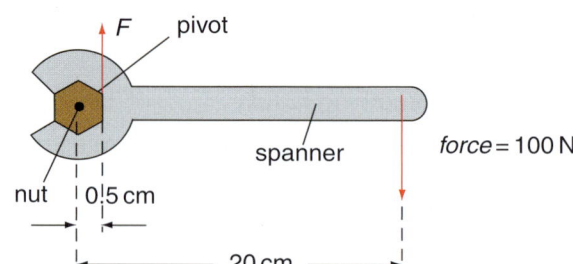

  a Calculate the moment of the 100 N force about the pivot.

  b If the 100 N force can just turn the nut, calculate the size of force F.

  c Why can you tighten a nut much more tightly with a spanner than you can with your fingers?

9 Here are some forces acting on a beam.

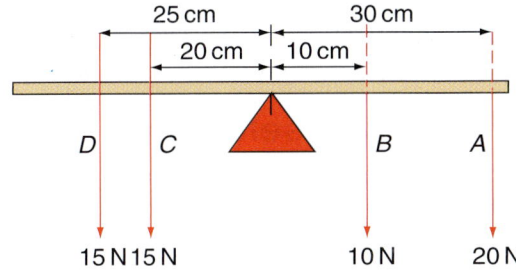

25 cm   30 cm
20 cm 10 cm
D   C   B   A
15 N 15 N   10 N   20 N

a Work out the moments of all of the forces.

b Is the beam balanced? If not, which way would it tilt?

c Where would you move force *B* to make it balance?

10 Here is a diagram showing a helium balloon, a metre ruler and a fulcrum.

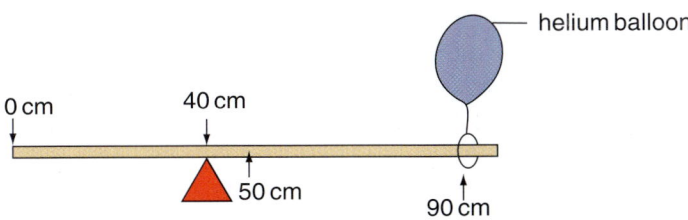

helium balloon

0 cm   40 cm

50 cm

90 cm

a State two forces that are acting on the ruler (other than the force from the fulcrum). Where do these forces act and in what direction?

b If the weight of the ruler is 3 N and the ruler is balanced, what is the upthrust on the balloon?

11 Here is a simplified diagram of an elbow joint.

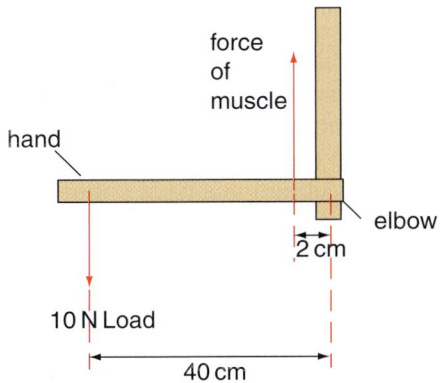

force of muscle

hand

elbow

2 cm

10 N Load

40 cm

What force does the muscle have to exert in order for the hand to hold a 10 N load?

12 How do tightrope walkers use a horizontal bar to keep themselves from falling off when they wobble sideways?

Answers

1 Inheritance and cloning

1 They are the sex cells that join together in fertilisation.

2 Sperm have tails that enable them to swim and lots of mitochondria to give them energy; egg cells have a lot of cytoplasm to feed the embryo until it is capable of feeding from the mother.

3 They are sequences of DNA that define a particular characteristic and found in the nucleus of a cell.

4 Half of your genome comes from each parent. Less than half comes from a particular grandparent.

5 a One gamete comes from the father and one comes from the mother. The genetic information from both gametes forms the new individual.

  b They might have inherited the same genes for certain characteristics but different genes for others.

  c Identical twins are formed when a fertilised egg splits into two and each new cell forms an embryo; non-identical twins are formed when two sperm fertilise two eggs.

  d Yes, if they inherit exactly the same combination of genes, but this is highly unlikely.

6 a The offspring is always tall when it inherits this gene.

  b Since the 'tall' gene is dominant, the parent must be tall if it is in possession of this gene.

  c They must both have one 'tall' gene and one 'dwarf' gene and must both pass on the 'dwarf' gene.

7 a It is an organism with identical genetic make-up to its 'parent'.

  b Take cuttings and grow them.

  c The amoeba reproduces by splitting in half. Hence identical genes are passed on.

  d It is a clone of the organism that produced the nucleus.

  e Almost every cell (except the gametes) contains all of your genetic information.

  f It is very difficult to carry out without damaging the egg; there are also ethical reasons.

8 They manufacture proteins. The genetic code tells them what amino acids to use.

9 The DNA does not get altered so the mitochondria are clones of your mother's. You will ultimately be descended from the same female as the complete stranger.

10 The sex chromosomes are called X and Y. Your mother will have two X chromosomes and your father will have an X and Y chromosome. Therefore you will inherit either XY or XX. If you inherit XY you are male; if you inherit XX you are female.

2 Variation and selection

1 It is both. Availability of resources such as water, light and minerals will affect tree growth but there are also shorter and taller varieties of tree.

2 We have developed agricultural techniques to maximise their growth; we have selectively bred the larger growing varieties.

3 Wolves with a tamer nature were easier to domesticate; this characteristic was continuously selected and passed down the generations.

4 Breeds of the same species can mate and produce fertile offspring. Different species can't do this.

5 a This is the selection of certain characteristics over the generations due to the type of environment.

  b These bacteria survive longer and so are more likely to reproduce, passing on this characteristic. Some bacteria might cause infections that can't be treated.

  c They reproduce much more quickly.

  d Offspring that are born with a particular characteristic that is helpful for their environment are more likely to survive and reproduce. As this process continues, the characteristics become more and more tuned to an environment.

  e Finches become adapted to their particular environment (e.g. shape of beak) and can be very different to other finches in different environments.

6 a Keep on selecting, and breeding from, offspring that show this trait.

  b Resistance to disease.

7 a Humans have chosen particular characteristics that they want to develop through breeding. Different groups of humans have chosen different characteristics.

  b This characteristic was deliberately chosen as less-docile large dogs are dangerous.

8 a Take cuttings of the geraniums and grow them.

  b Clones have identical characteristics that would not change over generations.

  c Encourage geraniums with different characteristics to reproduce. Select offspring with features you want and encourage those to reproduce and so on.

9 a By providing genetic material in his sperm.

   b No horse is perfect – you need to match the strengths of the stallion with the weaknesses of the mare.

   c Humans used the stronger breeds for power. They are no longer needed.

10 a Both involve changing the genetic make-up of the offspring to enhance a characteristic. GM crops have had their genes manipulated directly.

   b GM crops might reproduce with other crops, with unknown consequences for the ecosystem.

   c Improved food yield; increased resistance to disease.

11 A mutation. If this leads to beneficial characteristics the organism will survive and reproduce.

12 They eat grass. Therefore the energy stored in the grass can be passed onto humans (who can eat goats but who can't digest grass directly).

3 Keeping fit and healthy

1 Being fit means you return back to normal quickly after exertion; being healthy means you haven't got any diseases and your body is functioning normally.

2 Glucose + oxygen → water + carbon dioxide (+ energy); $C_6H_{12}O_6 + 6O_2 \rightarrow 6H_2O + 6CO_2$.

3 Glucose originally comes from food and is extracted through the digestive system; oxygen comes from the air which is absorbed by the lungs. Both are transported by the bloodstream (pumped by the heart) to the cells where respiration takes place. The waste products dissolve in the blood and are pumped to the lungs by the heart. They pass through into the air and are breathed out.

4 Both involve bursting blood vessels. A stroke is in the brain but a heart attack is in the heart.

5 a The heart.

   b The transport of oxygen is not efficient.

   c The vessels have a smaller cross-sectional area and resist the flow of blood more.

   d They might rupture.

6 a Smoke contains the drug nicotine.

   b They propel mucus up the airways to the mouth where the mucus is swallowed.

   c The mucus moves down into the lungs and needs to be coughed out.

   d The alveoli become damaged, reducing the surface area of the lungs; air passages become inflamed and therefore narrower.

   e Cancer.

   f Carcinogenic chemicals can pass from the mother's bloodstream through the placenta into the fetal bloodstream.

7 a The diaphragm contracts and flattens and the intercostal muscles expand the ribcage to give the chest a larger volume.

   b Breathing in; the diaphragm relaxes on breathing out.

   c You need more oxygen in a given time so you need to breathe in at a faster rate and transport the oxygen to the cells more quickly.

8 a It provides support for the body; it protects the vital organs; it contains joints to allow movement.

   b Tendons are connected between muscle and bone; ligaments are connected between bone and bone and hold the bones together at a joint.

   c It lubricates the joint to allow it to move easily.

   d Muscles can only contract so can only move the bone one way. The bone needs to move two ways, so you need two muscles.

   e Lifting up: biceps contracts and triceps relaxes; moving down: biceps relaxes and triceps contracts.

   f We could move our joints very quickly and therefore run fast.

9 a It respires anaerobically. Glucose breaks down and releases energy in the absence of oxygen. One of the by-products is lactic acid which leads to pain in the muscles.

   b Your body needs oxygen to convert the lactic acid into other harmless substances.

4 Diet and drugs

1 Carbohydrates, protein, fats, vitamins, minerals.

2 Diets with too much fat; not enough exercise. Changes in lifestyle have led to the popularity of fast food and easy meals. Modern entertainment is produced by computer games rather than active sports.

3 It impairs your judgement and reaction times leading to you taking unnecessary risks.

4 Addiction is the physical and/or psychological dependence on a drug. Tolerance is how much drug is needed before it has the desired effect.

5 a Change sugar levels in food depending on whether the blood sugar levels are too high or too low (most sufferers also need daily injections of insulin).

b More vitamin C, for example citrus fruits.

c Better balanced diet – less fat in particular.

d More iron in the diet.

e More fibre in the diet.

f More protein in the diet.

g Diabetes is not usually caused by a poor diet; anaemia is often associated with blood loss.

6 a 19.6, underweight; 31.1, obese; 27.8, overweight.

b They have lots of muscle tissue which is denser than fatty tissue.

7 a Men are generally bigger than women and have a higher water content.

b Pilots need to have much faster reactions to remain safe.

c 9 hours.

d It is scarring of the liver tissue; the liver plays a vital role in removing toxins from the body.

8 a It is a fake drug that has no pharmaceutical effect. They need to make sure that any differences aren't due to the patient simply thinking that they are being helped.

b The doctors can't influence the results by imagining that the drug is actually working (in the same way that a placebo has an effect).

c You need to make sure that the drugs are safe to be tested on humans.

9 a Hallucinogens and painkillers.

b Stimulant: cocaine; sedative: tranquillisers; hallucinogen: LSD; painkiller: heroin.

c People become dependent on the drugs and might resort to crime to obtain the money to buy the drugs.

10 a They are more harmful.

b When the benefits greatly outweigh the harm they can cause.

11 Physically dependent means that your body doesn't function 'normally' when the levels of the drug are too low; psychologically dependent means that you can't cope emotionally without the drug. Nicotine patches deal with physical dependency.

5 Photosynthesis

1 *Synthesis* means joining together and *photo* means light, so the reaction is the joining together of carbon dioxide and water through the action of light.

2 Oxygen: relights a glowing splint; carbon dioxide: turns limewater milky; starch: turns iodine solution blue/black.

3 Photosynthesis is the reverse reaction of respiration.

4 It is the total mass of living organisms.

5 a Carbon dioxide + water (+ energy) → glucose + oxygen; $6CO_2 + 6H_2O \rightarrow C_6H_{12}O_6 + 6O_2$.

b Light.

c It lowers the energy needed to make the reaction happen.

6 a Water and carbon dioxide.

b The tree takes minerals from the soil.

7 a So that you can test whether photosynthesis takes place during your experiment instead of before it.

b It gets used up in respiration.

c The iodine can't penetrate the cell walls.

d Boiling the leaves breaks the cells walls; the ethanol dissolves the chlorophyll and removes the green colour from the leaf.

e In a water bath.

8 a It is dissolved in the water.

b Measure how much oxygen is produced in a certain time for different light intensities.

c Temperature (the rate of photosynthesis depends on temperature); amount of pondweed (more pondweed – more oxygen).

d You could leave the experiment for long periods of time and continually collect data.

e The graph will rise with a positive gradient as light intensity increases but then become a straight horizontal line when the rate of photosynthesis is limited by other factors.

9 The plant is respiring and photosynthesising at the same rate.

10 It reacted with other chemicals (particularly iron) and it also dissolved in the water.

11 Oxygen cannot be in an atmosphere of its own accord – it is too reactive. Other process (such as life) must be putting it there.

6 Leaves and roots

1 The light energy reaches the tops of the leaves rather than the bottom so this is where photosynthesis takes place.

2 To collect as much light and carbon dioxide as possible.

3 They have a collection of tissues and they perform a specific task.

4 Water is a reactant in photosynthesis.

5　a It is a leaf that has areas containing chlorophyll and areas that don't.
　　b De-starch the plant, then let it photosynthesise for a few days. Boil the leaves and remove the chlorophyll using warm ethanol. Finally apply iodine solution. The iodine should turn blue/black where the leaves were originally green, showing the variegated pattern.
6　a They provide the cells with water.
　　b They take in the air to provide the carbon dioxide. This isn't needed during the night.
　　c They store the gases in the air.
　　d This prevents water escaping since it would evaporate too quickly in hot temperatures.
　　e So that it is easy for the carbon dioxide to reach the top of the leaf.
7　a So that it can be stored (starch is insoluble).
　　b Animals eat the fruits and spread the seeds via movement and excretion.
　　c They come from the minerals absorbed by the roots. Amino acids form proteins.
　　d The cell wall.
　　e To control the passage of chemicals to and from the cell.
8　a The hairs give it a large surface area with which to absorb water.
　　b They don't photosynthesise since there is no light in the soil.
　　c From the air trapped in the soil.
　　d To produce vital materials, e.g. nitrogen for proteins.
　　e The active transport needs energy; diffusion is a natural effect.
9　The xylem transports water from the roots to the leaves; phloem transports minerals and sugars up and down the plant. The blood supply is used to transport chemicals in the human body.
10　Carnivorous plants obtain their minerals from insects.

7 Food from plants

1　Omnivores.
2　They eat animals that eat animals that eat plants.
3　It gets more diluted since organisms need energy from food for everyday functions.
4　Since the energy gets more diluted, the biomass of each part of the food chain must be lower than the previous level to make the total population sustainable.

5　a For seed dispersal.
　　b A succulent fruit has much more water in it.
　　c Fertilisation of the egg.
　　d They contain a lot of sugar; sugar provides energy.
6　a e.g. wheat, barley, rye, oats and maize.
　　b Grass.
　　c Through selective breeding, offspring with the genetic make-up to produce bigger yields are selected and made to reproduce.
　　d To provide fibre and help our digestive systems to work efficiently and avoid constipation.
　　e We drink the milk from cows.
7　a e.g. beans, peas, lentils.
　　b We eat both fruit and seeds when we eat beans like runner beans or French beans; the others listed here are just seeds.
　　c They are a valuable source of protein other than meat and dairy products.
8　a Root.
　　b Flower.
　　c Leaf stalks.
　　d Grains.
　　e Grains.
　　f Tuber.
　　g Leaf bud.
9　We can't digest all of the parts. Some of them might be poisonous.
10　Eat animals that can digest the plants.
11　a Photosynthesis.
　　b Ingestion and egestion.
　　c Decomposition (by bacteria or fungi).
　　d Photosynthesis.
　　e Digestion.
12　The fruit does not grow from the flower but from surrounding tissues.
13　They have a symbiotic relationship with nitrogen-fixing bacteria that live in special root nodules. The bacteria convert nitrogen from the air into ammonia.
14　The potatoes form sprouts which grow into new potato plants.

8 Improving the yield

1　Light intensity; temperature; concentration of carbon dioxide.
2　The minerals and nutrients they need are provided by the decay of other organisms that have died.
3　An organism that kills unwanted pests.
4　Any plant that is growing in a place where it isn't wanted.

5 a To replace the minerals that have been taken from the soil by the crops.
   b From food eaten by the animals who produced the manure.
   c They are light and can be dropped onto fields where the crop is growing; they release the minerals straight away.
   d Nitrogen.
   e So that it doesn't wash off the fields and alter natural habitats.

6 a They compete for resources such as light and water.
   b A broad-spectrum herbicide kills a wide variety of plants. A selective herbicide only kills one type.
   c An advantage is that you minimise the amount of herbicide used. A disadvantage is that you might kill plants that don't need to be killed.
   d You could easily spray other areas by accident, killing wild plants.
   e Picking the weeds out of the ground by hand.

7 a They can eat the crops; they can help pollination; they can transmit diseases.
   b The level of pesticide becomes more concentrated as it passes up the food chain and could reach lethal levels in higher organisms such as birds.
   c These insects eat the pests that affect the crops, thus acting as a natural pesticide.

8 a So that you can make it grow quickly.
   b They kept the light intensity and the temperature constant.
   c It has an optimum value rather than just reaching a maximum limit and remaining there.
   d Too high a temperature will reduce the rate of photosynthesis whereas there is no such thing as too much light or too much carbon dioxide.
   e The low light would limit the rate of photosynthesis to such an extent that the temperature would have no effect unless it was very hot or cold.

9 It increases the temperature, aiding photosynthesis; it prevents animals from eating the crops.

10 They allow heat radiation from the Sun to pass through them but they reflect back heat radiation from the crops (which is at a different wavelength). Therefore the heat entering the greenhouse is more than the heat leaving and the greenhouse warms up.

11 Farmers can use machines to cultivate very large areas quickly.

12 Most populations of pests prefer one type of crop. Rotating crops prevents populations of pests from building up. Legume plants add nitrogen to the soil in the form of nitrates.

9 Metals and acids

1 On all of it apart from a small part on the right-hand side.
2 Mercury; no.
3 Iron, cobalt and nickel.
4 Hydrogen.
5 a They are shiny.
   b The atoms are packed closer together.
   c A crystal is a regular array of atoms; polycrystalline means they have lots of crystals.
   d Metals are much better at conducting heat.
   e No, although they all conduct better than non-metals. Graphite is a non-metal that conducts electricity.
   f They are strong; they are dense and so relatively heavy.
6 a It reacts violently.
   b Hydrogen; gives a squeaky pop in the presence of a glowing splint.
   c By evaporation.
   d Sodium chloride.
7 a i $Zn + H_2SO_4 \rightarrow ZnSO_4 + H_2$; ii $Zn + 2HCl \rightarrow ZnCl_2 + H_2$.
   b Salts.
   c Water.
   d The water makes the hydrogen atoms (ions) separate from the rest of the atoms in the acid.
8 a Potassium sulfate.
   b Add potassium to some sulfuric acid. Then evaporate the water – the potassium sulfate should crystallise out.
   c $2K + H_2SO_4 \rightarrow K_2SO_4 + H_2$.
9 Metal + acid $\rightarrow$ salt + hydrogen.
10 There is only one form of zinc chloride whereas you can get CO and CO_2 so you need carbon dioxide to distinguish it from carbon monoxide.
11 a It is the maximum possible amount you can obtain if everything works perfectly.

b The sulfate adds to the mass.

c $\frac{2}{3} \times 12.6 = 8.4$ g.

d The two reactants always react in the same proportion. There is only enough sulfuric acid to react with 3 g of sodium.

10 Other acidic reactions

1 It is a compound of a metal and oxygen.

2 It is a scale from 1 to 14 (usually) indicating the acidity of a solution. 1 is very acidic and 14 is very alkaline; a value of 7 indicates a neutral solution. The pH of a weak acid could be 4 and a weak alkali could have a pH of 9.

3 Indicators.

4 It comes from the chemical energy of the reactants (more specifically from the new bonds made).

5 **a** 60%.

  b 22%.

  c CO_2.

  d The release of heat.

  e Calcium carbonate is laid down as sediment at the bottom of the ocean where it gradually changes into limestone. As the limestone goes deep into the Earth's crust, the high temperatures and pressures turn it into marble.

  f Calcium carbonate + nitric acid → calcium nitrate + water + carbon dioxide.

  g It would increase.

6 **a i** H_2SO_4; **ii** HNO_3; **iii** HCl.

  b They all have hydrogen but they contain other different elements.

  c Potassium sulfate, potassium nitrate, potassium chloride.

  d No; the bonding is relatively strong.

7 **a** Copper oxide + sulfuric acid → copper sulfate + water.

  b Copper sulfate.

  c Apply heat.

8 **a** $Ca(OH)_2 + 2HNO_3 \rightarrow Ca(NO_3)_2 + 2H_2O$.

  b i Calcium nitrate; **ii** calcium hydroxide; **iii** nitric acid.

  c 7.

9 **a** Metal carbonate + acid → salt + carbon dioxide + water.

  b Metal oxide + acid → salt + water.

  c Alkali + acid → salt + water.

11 Reactivity of metals

1 It isn't very reactive and so other metals are very likely to displace it from its compounds.

2 The surface gradually becomes duller due to chemical reactions with the air.

3 It is much easier to extract bronze (an alloy of tin and copper) from rocks than iron.

4 Iron oxide. Iron reacts with oxygen (using salty water as a catalyst). It is a problem as rust easily erodes away leaving fresh iron to react with the air. Therefore iron structures gradually become thinner and weaker if they are allowed to rust.

5 **a** Sodium is a very reactive metal; gold hardly reacts at all.

  b The reaction with the air only happens at the surface.

6 **a** Concentration of hydrochloric acid and temperature.

  b Magnesium at the top and copper at the bottom.

  c Hydrogen; see if a lighted splint gives a squeaky pop.

  d See how much gas is produced in a given time. The metal that produces the most gas is reacting quicker and is more reactive.

7 **a** Li, Na, K.

  b Li – bubbles; Na bubbles vigorously and moves around on the surface of the water; K bubbles very vigorously and produces a flame.

  c Hydrogen; it is highly flammable.

  d Put some indicator in the solution and observe the colour.

  e K, Na, Li.

  f Rubidium and caesium; it is far too dangerous.

  g They are very reactive so combust easily. Their reaction with water is violent and would make the situation far worse.

  h It is less reactive.

  i Reactivity increases as you go down the group.

8 **a** The metal is reacting with oxygen to form a metal oxide.

  b Metal + oxygen → metal oxide.

  c It is more reactive.

  d No chemical reaction takes place.

9 It is shiny so can be seen easily; it doesn't dissolve in water so remains in the pan; it is dense so it sinks to the bottom of the pan; it is not reactive so is found as an element rather than a compound.

10 Place different metal electrodes in a salt solution. There is a small voltage between them. The bigger the voltage obtained, the bigger the difference in their reactivity.

12 Displacement reactions

1 It is a solution containing a dissolved compound. The compound can be formed by a metal displacing hydrogen from an acid.

2 It is a reaction in which one element replaces another less reactive element in a compound

3 Yes; the metal displaces the hydrogen.

4 You can use more reactive metals to displace the less reactive metals from the ore, but not the other way round.

5 a Potassium, sodium, calcium, magnesium, aluminium, carbon, zinc, iron, lead, hydrogen, copper, gold.
  b The most reactive elements are on the left.
  c Carbon and hydrogen.
  d Potassium.
  e Copper and gold; they are less reactive than hydrogen so wouldn't displace it.

6 a It is a mineral from which a metal can be profitably extracted.
  b The coal would burn in the air to form carbon dioxide and the coke would not form.
  c Carbon.
  d Carbon is more reactive than iron so coke could displace iron in a displacement reaction. This reaction occurs at a very high temperature.
  e Calcium is more reactive than carbon and so cannot be displaced by it.

7 a They are very difficult to break apart because they are very strongly bonded together.
  b The more stable the compound, the greater the amount of heat is given out.

8 a The iron is displacing the copper to form (green) iron sulfide. The displaced copper (brown) attaches to the nail.
  b Nothing; iron is less reactive than magnesium.
  c The green solution would turn colourless and iron would be deposited.

9 a Aluminium + iron oxide → aluminium oxide + iron.
  b $2Al + Fe_2O_3 \rightarrow 2Fe + Al_2O_3$.
  c There is a much larger surface area for the reaction to take place and the reactants are not separated from each other.
  d Heat, e.g. a magnesium fuse.

e The iron produced is molten and can be poured into the gaps.
f Copper is less reactive than iron so wouldn't displace it. Potassium would just be too dangerous.

10 It can be obtained cheaply.

11 Extracting iron uses a lot of energy but recycling it uses a lot less.

12 Aluminium oxide forms a thin protective layer that doesn't erode.

13 When metal salts dissolve in water, they split up into charged ions. The electrodes attract the positive metal ions one way and the negative non-metal ions the other.

13 Acidity in the environment

1 It is rain that is more acidic than it would be from natural effects.

2 This is the breaking up of rocks due to physical, chemical and biological processes.

3 Soils contain many tiny rock fragments that separated from rocks due to weathering.

4 Lichens don't like acidic conditions. Traffic fumes can cause acid rain.

5 a Carbonic acid, sulfuric acid and nitric acid.
  b Respiration of plants and animals.
  c Volcanoes emit sulfur dioxide.

6 a Carbon monoxide.
  b The carbon dioxide produced can cause acid rain.
  c Nitric acid must be more acidic than carbonic acid since it obviously does more damage (otherwise there would be no point in using the catalytic converter).

7 a Erosion is the wearing away of a material; corrosion is specifically the wearing away of materials due to chemical attack.
  b The product of its reaction (calcium hydrogen carbonate) is soluble and so is easily eroded.
  c Big cities produce more acidic rain due to air pollution. High temperatures speed up the chemical reactions.
  d No, since gold is much less reactive.

8 a The plants need the minerals to function properly.
  b It is in contact with the plant for a much longer time without draining away.
  c It is a base and so neutralises the acidity of the lakes. More acid rain falls, so the lakes become acidic again.

9 a The water draining through the soil.
  b From decaying plants and other organisms.
  c The water drains away taking the alkaline solution, leaving the soil very acidic.
10 The bacteria can replace the limestone that has eroded away.
11 The type of vegetation present (some decays into more acidic compounds than others); the types of minerals in the local rocks (with differing pH values); the structure of the soil – as in question 9, soils that drain easily are often acidic.
12 We are more aware that acid rain is a problem and we are trying to control emissions.

14 Air pollution and global warming

1 Since the Industrial Revolution there have been huge emissions of pollutants into the environment.
2 Global warming is the gradually increasing temperature of the planet. Climate change is a change in the weather possibly brought on by global warming.
3 It reduces the heat radiation leaving Earth in the same way that a greenhouse reduces heat radiation leaving its interior.
4 They are running out and are very useful for producing other materials.
5 a Oxygen.
  b It stops the UV light from harming us and other organisms.
  c They have damaged the ozone layer.
  d In aerosols.
  e The CFCs are still present in the ozone layer and they are not biodegradable.
6 a CO.
  b It prevents oxygen from attaching to the haemoglobin and so we quickly die through oxygen starvation.
  c You can't smell or see carbon monoxide.
7 It is a smoky fog. Laws have been made to reduce the amount of pollution in sensitive areas.
8 a So that the pollutants are released high up in order to dissipate effectively.
  b No; the same amount of pollution is emitted.
  c Opposite charges attract, so the soot collects on the positive plates. A hammer then hits the plates and the soot falls off to be collected at the bottom of the chimney.

9 a It is waste that can be broken down into harmless chemicals by bacteria.
  b It doesn't pollute the environment for as long as conventional waste.
10 a They let the heat radiation from the Sun through them but they reflect the heat radiation from the Earth back down to the surface.
  b Yes; most of the greenhouse effect is due to water vapour. It is an essential feature of the Earth's climate since temperatures would be too low for most life forms without it.
  c We have monitoring stations high up in the atmosphere (e.g. Mauna Loa in Hawaii).
  d Water expands in higher temperatures; land-locked ice melts and drains into the sea.
  e The scientists can get primary data about the relationship between global temperatures and carbon dioxide levels.
  f The temperature is changing all the time by much more than 0.6 degrees, so they had to make sure they were getting a true average.
11 No, they won't. When an ice cube melts, the water level remains the same. This is because the volume of ice below the waterline gets less as the ice melts, by exactly the same amount as the melted ice added to the water.
12 For example, the Sun's activity, changes in the Earth's orbit.
13 It is an ocean current which moves warm water across the Atlantic to the north of the UK. If this stopped, there is a chance that the UK climate would cool down.
14 The plants' life processes are triggered by changes in the climate. If animals that eat the plants arrive later than the fruits and nuts produced by plants, their food supply could diminish.

15 Chemical energy

1 a Exothermic.
  b Endothermic.
2 Heat energy is given out.
3 They are being formed.
4 When bonds are made, heat energy is given out; when bonds are broken, heat energy is absorbed.
5 The steam releases heat energy in order to condense into water at 100 °C. This is extra energy that the boiling water doesn't have and so it can burn you more.

6 a $2H_2 + O_2 \rightarrow 2H_2O$.
   b It takes up a large volume and it is highly explosive.
   c The product of its combustion in air is simply water.
7 a The more reactive the metal, the stronger the bonds it forms.
   b You would choose a salt of a metal with low reactivity and add a very reactive metal to displace it.
   c You need heat to break the bonds between the iron and oxygen atoms.
8 The particles are moving faster so collide with each other more frequently and get close enough to form bonds.
9 a Combustion.
   b The molecules on the left-hand side of the equation need splitting up so the atoms can rejoin in different combinations.
   c You need to break some bonds.
   d The heat given out when the bonds are made is more than the heat needed to break the bonds.
   e There are 3 carbon, 12 hydrogen and 8 oxygen atoms on each side.
   f In the first reaction there are twice as many oxygen molecules as methane molecules; in the second reaction there are $\frac{4}{3}$ as many oxygen molecules as methane molecules.
   g When there is not very much oxygen.
   h CO is carbon monoxide, Co is cobalt.
   i In the second reaction, carbon is produced; this is the soot.
10 a Respiration: glucose + oxygen → carbon dioxide + water (+ energy); photosynthesis: carbon dioxide + water (+ energy) → glucose + oxygen.
   b Photosynthesis is the reverse reaction of respiration. If both released energy, then by continually reversing the reaction you would liberate more and more energy from nowhere.
   c They use chlorophyll which acts as a catalyst.
11 a Zinc, since there is a larger voltage.
   b 0.32 V.

16 Making new materials

1 A chemical property refers to how an object makes and breaks bonds with other materials; a physical property refers to how an object behaves under all other conditions.
2 Mono: one; di: two; ate: with oxygen; poly: many.

3 a i SO_3; ii H_2O_2.
   b It easily liberates an oxygen atom to become water.
4 a The mass of the products = the mass of the reactants in all chemical reactions.
   b It would decrease.
   c i The hole allows the phlogiston to escape.
      ii The friction between the drill and the wood transforms mechanical energy into heat energy.
   d The air didn't have any phlogiston in it, so the phlogiston in the materials wanted to get there – hence the materials burned more brightly.
   e Oxygen.
   f They combine with oxygen atoms, which provide extra mass.
5 a From food and drink (apart from the atoms in the original fertilised egg).
   b Most return to the Earth via decomposition by bacteria.
   c The atoms move due to chemical reactions. Many chemical reactions require energy. The chemical reaction that produces energy, respiration, needs glucose which is formed by plants in photosynthesis using energy from the Sun. If there wasn't this source of energy, these chemical reactions couldn't take place.
6 It goes into the mass of the carbon dioxide and water vapour that are released in the reaction.
7 a 1.6 g.
   b Magnesium atoms are heavier than oxygen atoms.
   c $3.2 \div 2.4 = 1.33$ times as much magnesium. The proportion remains the same so there is 1.33 times as much magnesium oxide. Hence the amount of magnesium oxide is $1.33 \times 4 = 5.3$ g.
8 a There is an infinite number of combinations in which the amino acids can be joined together.
   b DNA provides the instructions for what amino acids are used to build particular proteins.
   c You have to draw the silk out slowly and you would need a lot of silkworms.
   d It was easy to mass-produce nylon and so its production was much cheaper than silk.
   e They needed to produce the material themselves without relying on imports from countries which might be cut off in the war. They couldn't grow the right trees in their climates so they had to find an alternative.

9
  a Two bonds are formed.
  b It carries on in a very long chain.
  c Break one of the double bonds. Then each of the two carbon atoms can join on to other ethene molecules by breaking one of their double bonds and so on.
  d For example, plastic bags, traffic cones, etc.

17 Energy and electricity

1 Chemical energy transforms into electrical energy.
2 Connect ammeters in series, and voltmeters in parallel across the component being tested.
3 It is the potential difference or the energy transformed per unit charge.
4 An energy transformation is energy changing from one form to another. Energy transfer is the change of location where the energy is having an effect – waves are a good example of energy transfer.
5
  a Electrical to kinetic.
  b Sound to electrical.
  c Electrical to heat.
  d Light to electrical.
6
  a The total energy before and after any action must be the same – although it can be in different forms.
  b Into heat, which eventually dissipates out into space.
7
  a A has used 100 J and B has used 40 J.
  b B is the most efficient since it produces the same amount of useful energy but wastes less.
8
  a It is a flow of electric charge.
  b None.
  c 0 V.
  d **i** 2.0 V; **ii** 2.0 V; **iii** 1.0 V; **iv** 1.0 V; **v** 0 V.
  e **i** 0.67 V; **ii** 1.33 V.
9
  a From chemical reactions in the potato.
  b The chemical reactions no longer have enough reactants.
  c You need metals of different reactivity to create a potential difference (voltage).
  d Potassium is highly reactive with water and therefore too dangerous.
10 The electric charges have electrical potential energy. The voltage is a measure of the difference in potential energy of the charges. It remains at 2 J until it gets to B. It then transforms 1 J into light and heat at the left-hand light bulb so it is left with 1 J at

C. It delivers the rest of its energy to the right-hand light bulb so it has 0 J at D. It then remains at 0 J until it gets to E.

18 Electricity and modern life

1 It is the same at every point.
2 It doesn't run out but appliances can't be portable.
3 230 V.
4 When you wanted a very dim source of light – e.g. a night light.
5
  a The energy from a primary fuel has been used to make the electricity; the electricity itself is used to provide energy and so is acting as a fuel.
  b It can easily be transformed into many different useful forms of energy.
  c It is easy to transport.
6
  a 60 A.
  b Some of the current is leaking to the Earth, which indicates a fault.
  c They are in parallel – otherwise, if one socket wasn't being used, none of the others would work.
  d It is measuring the electrical energy that you are using.
7
  a 4 kWh are used, so the cost is 40p.
  b 100 W = 0.1 kW, 20 minutes = 0.33 hours, so energy used = 0.1 × 0.33 = 0.033 kWh.
8
  a Electrical energy into light and heat.
  b The joulemeter clicked faster.
  c This light bulb is brighter and so transforms more energy in a given time. Therefore the joulemeter clicked faster.
  d Power is the rate of transformation or transfer of energy; that is, how much electrical energy transforms into light and heat every second.
  e The joulemeter would click more slowly since less energy is transformed into heat.
9
  a Kinetic energy into electrical energy.
  b It amplifies the magnetic field produced by the magnet.
  c Rotate the magnet faster; use a stronger magnet; have more coils.
10 They only want to produce as much electrical energy as people actually need. After an important TV event (such as a world cup football match) everyone gets up to put the kettle on and go to the toilet. This requires a sudden increase of electrical

energy (the water companies need electricity to pump the sewage if you're wondering why going to the toilet needs electricity!). Unless the electricity companies are producing the right amount, the system could be overloaded, resulting in widespread power cuts.

11 Power lines can transmit electricity with lower currents if the voltage is high. Low currents mean that the power lines don't heat up as much and are therefore more efficient. An electric shock is due to an electric current flowing through you. Birds don't get shocked because they do not form a complete circuit. However, flying a kite into a power line would give you a shock since the electric current can flow from the power line through the kite and down into the Earth (a circuit is formed since the power station is connected to the Earth as well),

19 Gravity and orbits

1 The force of gravity acting on it.
2 The mass is the amount of matter, which stays the same. Your weight, however, changes if you go into space.
3 It would fly off in a straight line.
4 We are much closer to the Earth.
5 a i 600 N; ii 5 N.
   b i 5 kg; ii 100 g.
6 a The Moon has less mass.
   b 100 N.
   c A 1.2 kg mass would have this weight on Earth. Six times this mass would have the same weight on the Moon so the answer is 7.2 kg.
7 a The mass is (2400 ÷ 10) × 6 = 1440 kg.
   b 32 000 ÷ 1440 = 22.2 N per kg.
8 a Towards it – so upwards but the direction and elevation depend on where you are on the Earth's surface (on the equator during one of the equinoxes it will be vertically upwards).
   b It would be pulling you equally in all directions. Since these forces balance out, you would feel weightless.
   c The Moon is much closer to the Earth, so Earth's gravity is stronger.
9 a It needs to produce a resultant force upwards. This can only happen if the thrust is bigger than the weight.
   b The weight of the rocket gets less due to the burning of the fuel and it also gets less since the

force of gravity decreases as it moves away from the Earth.
   c It continues at a constant velocity.
10 a Towards the centre of the circle.
   b It would fly off at a tangent.
   c Friction. The car might not be able to turn as tightly and skid off the road.
11 a Gravity; downwards.
   b It has a horizontal speed which isn't affected by any force.
   c It would travel further horizontally before it reached the ground.
   d It would go all the way round the Earth.
   e The force of gravity isn't as strong so they don't fall as fast.
12 It is larger at the North Pole than at the equator since you are closer to the centre of the Earth.
13 You would fall to the centre of the Earth, pass through and emerge at the other side but gravity would bring you to a halt. Then you would fall back again the other way. Therefore you would oscillate from one side of the Earth to the other.

20 Understanding the Solar System

1 The Earth.
2 The telescope.
3 It contradicted the teachings of the Church.
4 It can see objects more clearly without disturbances caused by the atmosphere.
5 a An orbit above the equator that has a period of 1 day.
   b Communications; they are always directly above the same part of the ground.
   c It circles round the Earth between the North and South Poles.
   d The force of gravity is much stronger.
   e As they orbit, Earth's surface rotates underneath them, so for each orbit they are over another strip of the surface.
   f Monitoring weather; spying.
   g The diagram should show the Earth, one horizontal circle around the equator but a long way out (geostationary) and one vertical circle around the Earth much closer (polar).
   h To collect scientific data about that planet.
6 a The stars rotate about a fixed point.
   b The stars themselves are rotating about this point.

c It is reflected light from the Sun.

d They moved slowly relative to the constellations.

7 a If it didn't then the model couldn't possibly be true.

b He made the planets go in little circles while orbiting.

c Because the model was no longer fitting the facts.

d Because it contradicted the teachings of the Church and the argument wasn't powerful enough to alter peoples' belief.

8 a He discovered four moons of Jupiter.

b We feel gravity pulling us to the centre of the Earth, so this must be at the centre of the Universe.

c He produced a theory of gravity that was consistent with all of the facts and made sense if the Sun was at the centre.

9 The Sun is orbiting the centre of the Milky Way galaxy, which contains billions of other stars. There are billions of galaxies in the Universe separated by vast distances.

10 Pluto is a lot smaller than people originally thought. There are other Pluto-sized objects orbiting the Sun further out.

11 When the planet Uranus was discovered its orbit seemed to be affected by the gravity of another object further out. By using Newton's equations people worked out the position of the new planet and Neptune was discovered.

12 A supermassive black hole; the motion of objects affected by its gravity.

21 Speed, distance and time

1 Average speed = distance ÷ time.

2 Faster.

3 1000 m; 3600 s.

4 $30 \times 3600 = 108\,000$ km/h.

5 $1200 \div 3600 = \frac{1}{3} = 0.33$ (2 d.p.) km/s.

6 a 36 000 m/h.

b 10 m/s.

c 0.2 km/s.

d 72 m/s = 259 200 m/h = 259.2 km/h.

e 144 km/h = 144 000 m/h = 40 m/s.

f 20 m/s = 72 000 m/h = 72 km/h.

7 a 10 m/s.

b The first bike was in front since the average speed of the second bike must be less than

10 m/s at this point if it continues to accelerate right to the end.

8 I will have walked twice as far so we must meet 4 km away from my house.

9 The time would be too short, so the speed would be too high.

10 a Speeding up.

b 19.6 cm/s and 39.2 cm/s.

c No; you would need the distance and the time between the two light gates. (The average of the two speeds you calculated would only be the average speed if the glider was accelerating at a constant rate.)

d It is an average speed over the distance of 2 cm.

11 a The faster the speed, the bigger the force which turns the metal drag cup against the pull of the spring and moves the pointer to show a higher speed.

b It measures the speed at a point since it does not rely on a distance and a time measurement.

22 Forces and motion

1 A force from the engine makes the car accelerate.

2 The mass is bigger, so the acceleration is less for the same maximum force.

3 It has more resistance; make your body more streamlined.

4 This is the constant speed that an object reaches when it is falling to the ground.

5 Upthrust is a buoyancy force due to pressure. It does not depend on the motion of the object.

6 a Air resistance.

b The size of the force is very small.

c The brakes apply a frictional force that is larger than air resistance.

d The frictional force from the brake pads is larger than the friction between the tyres and the ground, so the tyres begin to slip.

7 a More.

b Make the engine produce a bigger force; reduce the mass of the car; make the car more streamlined.

c Air resistance increases until it is the same size as the maximum force of the engine.

d No, since the maximum speed depends on the maximum force of the engine which is unaffected by mass. However, a heavier car would take longer to reach its maximum speed.

8 a It accelerates at a decreasing rate until it reaches constant speed.
  b Weight acts downwards; air resistance acts upwards.
  c Weight doesn't depend on speed; air resistance increases as speed increases.
  d Air resistance is larger.
  e They are the same size but in opposite directions.
  f 5 s; 2 m/s.
  g i It would reach a lower terminal velocity much earlier (all of the graph would be lower than the line; **ii** it would reach a higher terminal velocity much later (all of the graph would be higher than the line).
9 a Air resistance is bigger than the weight.
  b The weight stays the same; air resistance reduces until it is the same as the weight.
  c A parachute.
  d The temperature would be far too high and the parachute would burn up.

23 Pressure

1 Pressure = force ÷ area.
2 At right angles to it.
3 The water pressure increases.
4 Hydraulic systems use liquids; pneumatic systems use gases.
5 a $10 \div (2 \times 1) = 5 \text{ N/cm}^2$.
  b $10 \div (2 \times 4) = 1.25 \text{ N/cm}^2$.
6 For example, sharp rhinoceros horn, large camel feet.
7 a Air can compress.
  b 40 N/m^2.
  c $40 \times 2 = 80 \text{ N}$.
  d 40 times.
8 a Too high, tyre might rupture; too low, tyre might wear excessively leading to a blow-out.
  b This reduces the pressure on a given tyre.
  c Flat tyres reduce the pressure on the snow and increase the area in contact with the snow.
  d A large radius means that the tractor can cope with rough terrain; wide tyres reduce the pressure so tractors don't sink into the mud so much.
9 a Gas syringe.
  b The volume stays the same but the pressure increases.

10 Pressure increases with depth; it acts in all directions.
11 a i Upwards; **ii** downwards.
  b Pressure upwards is bigger than the pressure downwards (since it is deeper in the water). Therefore there is a resultant force upwards.

24 Levers and moments

1 Force × (perpendicular) distance to the pivot.
2 For an object to balance, the total moment of all of the forces turning in one direction must be equal to the total moment of all the forces turning in the opposite direction.
3 To increase the turning effect of the force.
4 You apply a small force over a large distance to produce a large force over a small distance.
5 $150d = 200 \times 15, d = 20 \text{ cm}$.
6 Yes; the weights would be different but they would still be in the same proportion.
7 The gears act in a similar way to a spanner turning a nut. The lowest gear would be like holding the spanner the furthest away from the nut and the highest gear would be like holding the spanner near to the nut (which would turn the nut faster but would require more force).
8 a 2000 N cm.
  b $F \times 0.5 = 2000, F = 4000 \text{ N}$.
  c Your fingers would be closer to the pivot and therefore the force you need would be greater to produce the same turning effect.
9 a $A = 600 \text{ Ncm}, B = 100 \text{ Ncm}, C = 300 \text{ Ncm}, D = 375 \text{ Ncm}$.
  b No; it would tilt to the right.
  c The moment of B needs to be 75 Ncm, so B needs to be 7.5 cm away from the pivot.
10 a Upthrust from the balloon upwards, weight at centre of ruler downwards.
  b Distance from weight force to pivot = 10 cm, distance from balloon to pivot = 50 cm, $3 \times 10 = F \times 50, F = 0.6 \text{ N}$.
11 200 N.
12 If they wobble one side of the wire, they push the bar to the other side, so the moment due to the bar balances the moment due to their weight.